W9-BAG-706

FOR CHRIST'S SAKE

**End Sexual Abuse
in the Catholic Church ...
for Good**

FOR CHRIST'S SAKE

**End Sexual Abuse
in the Catholic Church ...
for Good**

Bishop Geoffrey Robinson

garratt
PUBLISHING

garratt PUBLISHING

Published in Australia by
Garratt Publishing
32 Glenvale Crescent
Mulgrave, Vic. 3170

www.garrattpublishing.com.au

Design and typesetting by Cristina Neri, Canary Graphic Design
Images: thinkstock.com
Printed in China by Tingleman

9781922152886

Cataloguing in Publication information for this title is available
from the National Library of Australia. www.nla.gov.au

CONTENTS

Introduction 1

PART ONE
Factors Contributing to Abuse 9

CHAPTER ONE
Moving From a Religion of Fear to a Religion of Love 10

CHAPTER TWO
Moral Immaturity 22

CHAPTER THREE
Sexual Morality 47

CHAPTER FOUR
The Male Church 64

CHAPTER FIVE
A Culture of Celibacy 74

CHAPTER SIX
The Mystique of the Priesthood 81

CHAPTER SEVEN
Lack of Professionalism 89

CHAPTER EIGHT
Unhealthy Living Environment 104

PART TWO

Factors Contributing to the Poor Response   109

CHAPTER NINE

Right Beliefs v Right Actions   110

CHAPTER TEN

Papal Infallibility and Prestige   118

PART THREE

Enabling a Healthy Response   125

CHAPTER ELEVEN

The College of Bishops   126

CHAPTER TWELVE

The *Sensus Fidei* of the Whole Church   130

CHAPTER THIRTEEN

A New Council for a New Church   134

CHAPTER FOURTEEN

The Voice of the People of God   139

Petition for a Council   141

APPENDIX

Practical Suggestions   143

INTRODUCTION

If any of you put a stumbling block before one of these little ones who believe in me, it would be better for you if a great millstone were hung around your neck and you were thrown into the sea.

(MARK 9:42)

And yet, despite these words, thousands of priests and religious brothers worldwide have sexually abused minors, causing massive and lifelong harm.

When they first entered the seminary or novitiate, most of them were idealists, filled with enthusiasm for the message of Jesus and a desire to make the world a better place. Instead they have ended up violating every precept of Jesus, every teaching of the Church they profess to love, and every criterion of the most basic human decency.

There is an ancient saying: *corruptio optimi pessima* or, 'the corruption of the best is the worst'. If those who start out with the highest ideals fall, there is no limit to the depths they can fall to.

When so many people act this badly, we can no longer limit our blame to the individuals, but must also look for factors within the very culture of the Church that have contributed. And when so many authorities in the Church have attempted to conceal the abuse, or treated victims of abuse as though they were an enemy of the Church, we must again look for systemic factors behind such behaviour, factors that are part of the very culture of the Church.

Recently, a group of experts in advertising and public relations was asked what steps it might suggest to present the religion of Islam in the best light. Among the ideas suggested were: encouraging the bulk of moderate Muslims to speak up and dissociate themselves from the terrorists and fundamentalists, using women wherever possible as spokespersons, and identifying the one or two central ethical values at the heart of Islam and showing how ordinary Muslims live these values in their lives.

They were then asked to do the same for the Catholic Church. They discussed this for some time, but eventually said that, as long as the massive weight of the sexual abuse scandal was tied around the neck of that Church, there was really nothing they could suggest. Any talk of a 'new evangelisation' would be a waste of time. Indeed, any attempt to get back to 'business as usual' while the abuse scandal remained would be positively counterproductive.

Millions of good Catholics have been deeply disillusioned, both by the revelations of widespread abuse, and even more by what they have perceived as the defensive, uncaring and unchristian response on the part of those who have authority in the Church and claim to speak in God's name. The effects on the Church have already been massive and the poison will continue to eat away at the very foundations of the Church for as long as the issue remains.

On the other hand, if the Church really did confront the entire issue of sexual abuse with total honestly, ruthlessly uprooting anything and everything that may have contributed to either abuse or the poor response to abuse, this would in fact be the best possible evangelisation it could carry out, and would have far more effect than any more conventional form of evangelisation.

All the evidence available says that the number of offences in this field has fallen greatly, and some might be tempted to think that the problem has, therefore, gone away and no longer needs to be thought about. The sad fact, however, is that the major reason for the fall in the number of offences has been naked fear—fear of being arrested and sent to prison, fear of the walk of shame in handcuffs before the television cameras, fear of the total and permanent destruction of one's good name before all the people one has ever known.

It is obviously good that the number of offences has fallen, irrespective of the motive. And yet an improvement based largely on fear is surely not good enough as a total answer to the matter. Surely we need to look more deeply at any contributing factors within the Church, and eliminate them.

There are three major tasks to be performed in eradicating sexual abuse from the Church:

- identifying and removing all offenders
- reaching out to and assisting all victims/survivors

- identifying and overcoming the causes of both abuse and the poor response to abuse.

I have been involved in the first two fields for the last eighteen years and, in my position as a retired bishop not looked upon with favour by those in authority, I don't know that there is much more I can do. So I am here turning to the third element of identifying and overcoming the causes of both abuse and the poor response to abuse. We must have priorities in the work to be done, and for me the first priority will always be that of preventing abuse. Once abuse has occurred, anything we do will always be inadequate, so the only real solution is to prevent abuse happening in the first place.

I believe that it is in this field of preventing abuse that the greatest failure of the Church is to be found. The work of identifying and eradicating all the factors that may have contributed to abuse—and to the poor response—has not been done and, indeed, there has not even been a public call from the Pope for it to be done. There is a crying need that it should be done now and with a sense of great urgency. All levels of the Church must cease to simply 'manage' the problem and instead seek to confront it head-on, identifying and changing anything and everything that needs to be changed. Only then will the Church regain some measure of credibility.

Since the subject is vast, there are a number of further comments that I need to make to specify and limit the purpose and scope of this book.

I speak of factors that 'may have contributed' to either abuse or the poor response to abuse. I freely admit that I do not have scientific proof that each of the factors I shall mention has contributed and I cannot have an exact knowledge of the extent to which each has contributed. If we were to demand such proofs, however, I believe we would merely be looking for an excuse to do nothing, and that cannot be good enough. If an element in the Church can be shown to be unhealthy, we should remove it anyway, especially if we can see a clear connection between that factor and the whole phenomenon of abuse.

There are some causal factors that are common to all offenders and others that are particular to each individual offender. In between these two, there are unhealthy factors within particular societies or organisations that can foster a culture in which abuse will more easily occur, or can compound the problem by contributing to a poor response. It is this culture within the Catholic Church that will be the particular focus of this book.

Needless to say, the Church must also look at broader factors in modern society that may have contributed to abuse. It might be argued, for example, that the more open portrayal of sex and the more liberal attitudes towards sex in modern Western society have led some priests to think that they too should benefit from these easier sexual attitudes. Any study of factors external to the Church, however, must never be to the exclusion of factors internal to the Church. Indeed, because the Church can change the latter in a way it cannot change the former, it must give particular attention to the internal factors, and it is these factors internal to the Church that I shall look at in this book.

Abuse is most likely to occur when the three elements of unhealthy psychology, unhealthy ideas and unhealthy living environment come together.[1] Many studies have been done concerning unhealthy psychological elements and I do not have the competence to add anything to what the specialists have said on this topic.[2] On the other hand, much remains to be done concerning unhealthy ideas and unhealthy living environments, and I hope that in these fields I may have more to offer.

I suggest that the major reason why the Church has not yet seriously looked at causes of abuse is that it fears that any serious and objective study of the causes of abuse would lead to a demand for change in a number of practices, attitudes, laws and even teachings within the Church, and it is quite unwilling to do this. In studying abuse, we must be free to follow the argument wherever it leads, and we must not impose in advance the limitation that our study cannot demand change in any teaching or

---

[1]   David Ranson, 'The Climate of Sexual Abuse', *The Furrow*, 53 (July/August 2002), pp. 387–397.

[2]   For a summary of the point psychology has reached, and for nineteen pages of bibliography on the subject, see 'Child Abuse: A Review of the Literature', The John Jay College Research Team, Karen J Terry, principal investigator and Jennifer Tallon, primary researcher. See also 'The Nature and Scope of the Problem of Sexual Abuse of Minors by Catholic Priests and Deacons in the United States', a Research Study conducted by the John Jay College of Criminal Justice. Both documents may be found on the website of the United States Conference of Catholic Bishops at http:/www.usccb.org/ocyp/webstudy.shtml

law. We must admit that there might be elements deep within the 'Catholic culture' that have contributed either to abuse or to the poor response to abuse.

Most of the cases of abuse that have come to light occurred a number of years ago and most of the offenders received their upbringing and training decades before that. The factors that led them to abuse may not exist in quite the same way or to the same extent today. Despite this, I shall study these factors, for it would be extremely dangerous to assume that any such factors had disappeared and no longer applied.

Priests and religious have many things in common, but they also have their differences. To be accurate concerning both groups in every statement I make would not be possible, and I feel that I would run the serious danger of making false statements about religious. Because of my personal experience, I shall here limit myself to speaking about priests, allowing religious to adapt my thoughts to their own situations.

This book is a continuation of the book that I published in 2007: *Confronting Power and Sex in the Catholic Church, Reclaiming the Spirit of Jesus*. I have repeated a certain amount of material from that book, but this book goes well beyond that one in the specific field of identifying causes of abuse.

I have been supported by many people in the writing of this book. I express special thanks to Sr. Evelyn Woodward RSJ and to Tony and Gerardine Robinson for their helpful and constructive comments. I thank Fr. Michael Whelan SM and all the members of Catalyst for Renewal for their encouragement. I thank Gary Eastman, Tony Biviano and all the staff at Garratt Publishing for their assistance over many years and their enthusiasm for this book. I thank all those many people who have been calling out for a more radical response to sexual abuse.

Above all, I thank all the victims of abuse who had the courage to come forward and tell their stories. If serious change ever occurs within the Church, the credit must go overwhelmingly to them.

PART ONE

Factors Contributing to Abuse

CHAPTER ONE

MOVING FROM A RELIGION OF FEAR TO A RELIGION OF LOVE

In any religion, everything without exception depends on the kind of god that is being worshipped. It is the single most important fact about any religious system, for every aspect of the system will flow from it.

Ideas concerning this god will inevitably contain many elements that arise only from human minds; for, while there is only one God, there are an endless variety of human misunderstandings of God. Unable to grasp the infinite God, human beings constantly create a lesser god in their minds and worship that god, a god who is usually a very large human being rather than the true God.

In particular, all people have both profound fears and profound longings within them, with the fears leading to ideas of an angry god, and the longings to ideas of a loving god, and then with these two forces in conflict within them.

We can perhaps see this more clearly by looking at some developments in moral thinking in the Bible, reflecting developing ideas of God.

SIX LEVELS OF MORALITY

In the moral journey of the people of Israel in the First Testament, we may distinguish a number of levels of moral thinking through which they gradually rose as their understanding of God changed and developed. I suggest six levels.

Level Six

In Genesis 4:23 a man named Lamech demanded seventy-seven fold vengeance for any wrong done to him. This is surely the most primitive level of relationships between people, the very starting point of a long journey, and it reflects a very primitive idea of God. If a whole society were to adopt this criterion of seventy-sevenfold vengeance for any wrong done, it would be condemned to an endless cycle of violence and chaos, and any technical progress it made would be repeatedly destroyed by the violence. It may be called the level of superiority and vengeance, for Lamech sought vengeance because he considered himself superior to all other people. No one is immune from falling back to this level at any moment. Indeed, whenever a serious wrong is done to us, it is often our first spontaneous reaction: 'If you hit me, I'll hit you twice as hard.'

Level Five

The people of Israel began to rise above the level of Lamech, but progress was slow, and the next level was no more than that of the well-known biblical saying: 'An eye for an eye, a tooth for a tooth.'[3] It was progress, for its force was: not seventy-seven teeth for one tooth—not even two teeth for one tooth—no more than one tooth for one tooth. It came from a time long before police forces and prisons, and so from a time when justice tended to be primitive, direct and physical. Far from requiring vengeance, it actually sought to restrict it. It may be called the level of justice without mercy.

In practice, however, it was still too close to the level of Lamech, and Mahatma Gandhi's comment on it was: 'An eye for an eye leaves the whole world blind.' It is the morality of 'getting even' ('He hit me first'). One is reminded of the chilling phrase attributed to Joseph Kennedy: 'Don't get mad; get even.' If humanity were to make serious progress, this rule would also have to give way to higher levels of morality.

Level Four

Throughout human history, people have related to other people on one of two bases: either the usefulness of others to themselves, or the essential dignity of others. Sadly, in all cultures and at all times (including our own) the first has tended to dominate, with people esteeming those who were useful to themselves while pushing to the margins of society those who were seen as 'not useful'. This is the moral level of self-interest based on the usefulness of others to oneself. Needless to say, most of our relationships are reciprocal, that is, we both give and receive, and this is a good thing. But it leaves the question of how we should

---

[3] Ex. 21:25, Deut. 19:21.

relate to both individuals and whole categories of people (e.g. the elderly, the Aboriginal people, homosexuals) who may in the eyes of some seem to have little to offer us. This level is reflected in many incidents in the Bible.

Self-interest will always be a powerful force in human relationships, but it is not an adequate basis for living in community. A community will inevitably disintegrate if it is based solely on self-interest and there is no mutual respect and concern.

Level Three

The third level is that of the Ten Commandments,[4] the level that best reflects the practical influence of the great Covenant between God and the people of Israel. This was the gigantic step upwards of the First Testament— reflecting a very different understanding of God—for the Ten Commandments were a serious attempt to base human relationships, not on the usefulness of others to ourselves, but on their essential dignity and on the rights that flow from this dignity. It may be called the level of respect for dignity and the rights that flow from dignity. Five consecutive commandments call for respect for one's neighbour's dignity as a human being. In the first four they do this by demanding respect for:

- life and physical integrity (you shall not kill)
- the relationships that make life worth living and give

---

[4] Ex. 20:1–17; Deut. 5:6–21.

it meaning (you shall not commit adultery)
- material goods (you shall not steal)
- a good name in the community (you shall not bear false witness).

Within the Catholic Church, a whole world of teaching on all aspects of sex is usually given under the commandment concerning adultery. I believe that this is a restrictive understanding and I suggest that this commandment should rather be seen in terms of respect for the relationships that give life meaning.

There would be little quarrel about the importance of life, possessions or a good name; but the Ten Commandments insist that we add relationships to the list, for much of our life depends on them. Furthermore, just as 'you shall not kill' includes 'you shall not wound or harm physically in any way,' so not harming the relationship of marriage through adultery includes not harming any relationships that are important to people in making meaning in their lives e.g. relationships with parents or children or siblings or friends.

I suggest that these four commandments are meant to be taken together, for when taken as one whole, they are a powerful affirmation of one's neighbour's dignity. If one respects any three of the four, but violates the fourth (e.g. relationships), this is not a 75% success, but a basic failure to respect one's neighbour.

In the fifth of the series, the commandments forbid even desiring to harm one's neighbour ('You shall not covet your neighbour's house; you shall not covet your neighbour's wife, or male or female slave, or ox, or donkey, or anything that belongs to your neighbour').

There is a powerful new understanding of God in the idea of an essential dignity in every human being that demands respect and that gives rise to binding rights.

As well as being a great step forward, the Ten Commandments are also the essential basis on which any higher level must be built, for it is impossible to truly love another person unless one first has a genuine respect for the dignity of that person and the rights that flow from this dignity.

Level Two

The third level was based on negative commandments: 'You shall not'; that is: 'Because you respect your neighbour's dignity, do no harm.' The second highest level requires that we not merely do no harm, but also do positive good to our neighbour. If I respect you as my equal, I will at least do you no harm and I will wish to see you given all that belongs to you by right. If I add love to respect, I will wish for all that is good for you and that is within my power to give you, even when you have no strict right to it. In other words, if I respect you, I will ask: 'Do you have a right to this?' If I love you, I will ask only: 'Do you need it and do I have it to give?' It is the level of love built on respect and reflects the god of the Golden

Rule: 'Love your neighbour as you love yourself',[5] or 'in all things treat others as you would like them to treat you.'[6]

The beatitudes of Jesus start here but then continue into the highest level of morality.

Level One

The highest level is also based on love, but this time on God's love for us. It is the level of the actions of Jesus: 'I give you a new commandment: love one another ... as I have loved you.'[7] It includes the idea of loving even our enemies.[8] For Christians, it reflects the God who gave totally-of-self in Jesus. Some might think that this level is a mere ideal that human beings could never live up to and that they can ignore in practice. Just occasionally, however, a story appears on our television screens e.g. of a stranger running into a burning house to rescue children. To do this involves far more than loving as one loves oneself; it is a genuine rising up to love as God loves. None of us will ever know whether we are capable of this level of heroism until we are faced with the test, and then we might surprise ourselves. Surely an overwhelming majority of parents rise to this level at many critical moments in their child's life, for there are many moments when they must love their child, not as they love themselves, but more than they love themselves.

---

[5] Lev. 19:18.
[6] Matt. 7:12.
[7] John 13:34.
[8] Matt. 5:43.

There is no one who cannot fall back to the sixth or lowest level at any moment, but there is also no one who is not capable of rising to the highest level. Whenever we fall back to one of the lower levels, we fall back to the understanding of God that goes with that level. Whenever we rise to one of the higher levels, we rise to the understanding of God that goes with that level.

Frequent examples of all six of these levels of morality are found in the Bible. There were, of course, steps backwards as well as forwards, but in these six levels of morality there is the story of the communal journey of the people of Israel, and it can become the story of the personal journey of each of us.

Because it is a journey, Jesus himself did not disdain less-than-perfect levels and on occasions appealed to self-interest.

> When you are invited by someone to a wedding banquet, do not sit down at the place of honor, in case someone more distinguished than you has been invited by your host; and the host who invited both of you may come and say to you, 'Give this person your place,' and then in disgrace you would start to take the lowest place. But when you are invited, go and sit down at the lowest place, so that when your host comes, he may say to you, 'Friend, move up higher'; then you will be honored in the presence of all who sit at table with you.[9]

In reading the Bible, it is a mistake to read the words as though they were in every case God's direct words to us

---

[9] Luke 14:8–10.

today. The Bible is the story of a journey, with a beginning, a middle and an end. Lamech may be taken as representing the beginning of that journey, and Jesus Christ is its end, with everything else representing some stage in-between. To appreciate any particular statement, we need to assess where it belongs in the journey of the people of Israel. And we need to assess the kind of God that is being reflected by and worshipped in that statement at that particular point in the long journey. There is a vast difference in the understanding of God between, for example, the words of the prophet Micah: 'Act justly, love tenderly, and walk humbly with your God',[10] and the story of God allegedly slaying 70 000 innocent people because King David had carried out a census of the people.[11]

RISING TO HIGHER LEVELS

Even though Jesus was the end of that journey, and we live in the time after Jesus, the journey still continues for us as we seek to purify our personal ideas of God. Human ideas of God will always be infinitely inadequate, though some ideas can at least assist growth, while others will hinder it.

To promote growth, we must move:

- from a god about whom we use many words to a stunned awareness of an 'otherness' beyond the reach of either imagination or language
- from a god who is contained within a book or the

---

[10] Mic. 6:8.
[11] 2 Sam. 24:15.

teachings of a human authority to a god who cannot be contained by any created thing

- from a god religious authorities can possess, package and dispense to others to a god of infinite surprise
- from limited human ideas (e.g. an elderly white male ruler) to a god who is above all limitations
- from an attitude that we will believe only in a god who agrees with us on all major matters to an attitude of profound humility before our own ignorance
- from a god greatly concerned with glory and majesty to a god not standing on dignity and not threatened by anything human beings can do, but caring passionately about what we do to each other, to ourselves and to the community
- from a god whose glory is to be found in our obedience to a god whose glory is to be found in our growth
- from an angry god, not to a god of soft love, but to a god who, out of love, wants our growth and, like a good parent or teacher, is not afraid to challenge us to grow
- from a religion in which beliefs, moral rules, worship and membership of an institution or human community holds first place to a religion in which a love-relationship with God holds first place
- from a commercial relationship with a god whose rewards can be earned by doing right things to a love-relationship with a god who is pure gift

- from a relationship in which we are firmly in charge and determine exactly what part God shall be allowed in our lives to a love-relationship of total giving
- from a god who demands that we bridge the gap between us to a god who always takes the first step and comes to us.

The Catholic Church is so vast and its history so varied that all of the ideas just mentioned, both good and bad, have had their place. There are many beautiful statements about a loving god and many examples of individuals whose lives reflected such a god in ways that had a deep impact on those who met them.

Sadly, there has also been a long history of the angry god, with the Inquisition being merely the most glaring example. Coercion of many kinds, including torture, has had its place in an institution that should have reflected the example of Jesus.

The very structure of the Church, with a monarchical Pope insisting on obedience and using coercive means to ensure conformity, means that the angry god is never far away. At every level of the Church, many Catholics experience this as the pervasive and dominant atmosphere.

This has created a Church in which, despite the talk of love, practice has been based too much on fear rather than love, and authorities have always had the support of the angry god for their words and actions.

Spirituality has too often been understood in the negative sense of self-denial, self-abasement and rejection of the 'world', and the Christian life has too often been seen as consisting overwhelmingly in right behaviour before a judgemental god. A constricting guilt has played too large a part in the lives of too many people. These are unhealthy ideas that have too often created an unhealthy atmosphere and contributed to unhealthy actions.

To change all of this will require far more than a beautiful statement about God's love. It will require a careful look at all aspects of the Church at every level, and the changing of everything that reflects the angry god—from finger wagging Popes, to priests who convince themselves that they listen to the people but always manage to get their own way in the parish, to the widespread lack of belief in and respect for conscience. This will be a massive task, but the rest of this book will make it clear that the angry god is to be found beneath most of the other factors I shall speak of. To change the culture while leaving the angry god in place is a contradiction in terms, for too much of the culture is built on the angry god. This is the first chapter, for I believe it is the single most important change that is needed if the scourge of sexual abuse is to be confronted and ended ... for good. Catholics of the future must live predominantly out of love rather than out of fear.

Believing in a primitive and angry god is unhealthy, and unhealthy actions such as sexual abuse can grow out of this unhealthy culture.

CHAPTER TWO

MORAL IMMATURITY

According to Webster's dictionary, morality is 'the quality of an action as conforming to or deviating from the principles of right conduct.' This is the most common meaning of the word 'morality' in the world today. In this understanding, morality is about performing right actions and avoiding wrong ones. This approach to morality has two serious drawbacks.

The first is that it lacks a context, for it does not address the purpose we hope to achieve by doing right actions, that is: why we should want to do good or be good.

The second difficulty is a corollary of the first, for the definition does not face the question of whether performing right actions, in and of itself alone, is an adequate means to achieve any purpose we might have, that is: whether doing right things, of itself alone, will make us good.

In its simplest terms, in any human enterprise, we first ask two questions: what goal do we wish to achieve and how shall we achieve that goal? The enterprise of living a moral life must address the same two questions.

THE PURPOSE OF MORALITY

In his novel, *A Burnt-Out Case*, Graham Greene depicts an unlovable character named Rycker.[12] Rycker had spent a number of years in the seminary studying to be a priest, but left before ordination and eventually drifted to live in a small village in the heart of Africa. In his own words:'At the seminary I always came out well in moral theology.'[13] In the book he constantly annoys the priests at the nearby leper colony with the artificial moral dilemmas he invents and loves to discuss for hours. Despite this, he is not a particularly moral person.

Among the mistakes he makes are:

- his attitude is negative, so he concentrates on not doing wrong things rather than actually doing something that might help someone
- he concentrates on the details of his life, i.e. specific actions, but ignores the plot, i.e. the whole direction his life is taking
- his model of morality is basically legal, i.e. obeying moral laws rather than truly imitating Jesus Christ
- he is motivated by fear more than love
- because of the kind of morality he practises, a debilitating guilt is never far from him
- while avoiding specific actions that are clearly forbidden, he is unloving towards his wife and the African people who work for him

[12] William Heinemann, London, 1961.
[13] op. cit., p.46.

- if asked about goals and means, his honest reply would have to be: 'The goal is that of getting into heaven; the means is that of not doing wrong things.'

The meaning given by Webster's dictionary to the word 'morality' is a restrictive one. It is part of the reason why being called a 'moral person' can have overtones of being judgemental, unloving and holier-than-thou.

The meaning of the word 'morality' should go far beyond not doing wrong things, for it must essentially include the purpose of:

- seeking to rise above ourselves and our own self-interest and to act on behalf of others
- seeking to act in accordance with what is deepest within ourselves
- seeking to open ourselves to truth, reality and life
- seeking to become more authentically ourselves
- seeking to grow to become all we are capable of being
- seeking to base our lives on justice and love.

In this life we are called to become all we are capable of being, all God invites us to be. If we wish to do this, we must try to live at the higher end of the six levels of morality I spoke of in the last chapter: on the bases of respect and love.

THE RESPONSE OF LOVE

The story of Jesus tells us that God is constantly saying to each one of us, 'I love you', and the only adequate response on our part is, 'I love you too'. From this response will flow many truths, many principles of right conduct and a genuine worship of God, but the response of love to the person comes first. Without the response of love to the person, the truths will become lifeless, the principles of right conduct will be burdensome tasks and the worship will be empty. With the response of love, the truths will come alive, the principles of right conduct will be the most natural things in the world and the worship will be life-giving. Right conduct divorced from the response of love will always be inadequate.

It follows from this that morality is essentially relational, for it is essentially about the kind of relationship we wish to have with God and, therefore, with other people. It is about the kind of god we worship: an angry god, a just god or a loving god. Despite all his studies, Rycker had failed to learn this simple truth and was caught in the worship of an angry god or—at best—a just god, but certainly not a loving god. He failed to see the fundamental truth that morality is about relationships more than individual actions. Christian morality cannot be simply about 'not doing wrong things'. It must be about building our relationship with God.

It follows that it is vitally important that morality and spirituality not be separated, so the saint is the truly moral person and the truly moral person will be a saint. The natural sense we all have within us that we should live morally must be seen as an invitation to holiness. If morality and spirituality are separated, morality will inevitably wither and die.

COMMANDMENTS AND BEATITUDES

If a family comes to live next door to me and I do no harm to them, I can hope that they will not become my enemies. But if I want them to be much more than 'not enemies', if I want a relationship of love and friendship, I must go well beyond 'doing no harm'. Our first moral duty is not to harm others and our second is to do what we can to help them. The first duty comes first, for it is foolishness to speak of helping people while we are actually harming them. The concern of the commandments is with this first duty and, because it comes first, we can never do away with it. Jesus never rejected the Ten Commandments: it is wrong to kill, harm life-giving relationships, steal legitimate possessions and damage a person's good name, and he proclaimed these truths constantly.

The Commandments, however, largely express negative requirements for growth ('You shall not…'). Even if we observe every negative commandment perfectly, this does not yet say very much about our spiritual state. It says what we have not done, but does not say that we have actually done anything positive to assist others. The negative commandments are a necessary foundation, for they ensure that we do not do positive harm to others, but they cannot in themselves build true moral and spiritual growth.

It was for this reason that Jesus, without doing away with the Ten Commandments, added to them the beatitudes.[14] To 'You shall not kill' Jesus added, 'Blessed are the peacemakers'. Not to kill or harm is the essential foundation, but true spiritual growth is to be found in doing all we can to create peace. To 'You shall not steal' Jesus added, 'Blessed are the poor in spirit'. Not stealing is the foundation, but true growth is to be found in the active seeking of spiritual values. There is a profound challenge to adopt a true Christian morality in the beatitude, 'Blessed are those who hunger and thirst for what is right, for they shall be filled', that is, blessed are those who desire all that is right and just and good, and who desire it with the same degree of intensity as a person dying of hunger desires food or a person dying of thirst desires water.

The beatitudes are not commandments, and we do not sin if we do not live up to their highest ideals, but it would be a total misunderstanding if anyone were to conclude that they are not, therefore, part of Christian morality. They are ideals rather than laws, but they are what has been called 'prescriptive ideals'; that is, we do fail if we totally ignore the ideals and make not the slightest attempt to strive towards them.

Any adequate understanding of Christian morality must include these ideas and purposes. If we take them away, morality will lack cogency in our lives and could become as empty and formalistic as it was in the life of Rycker.

---

[14] Matt. 5:1–12.

TAKING RESPONSIBILITY

As well as determining the goals we are seeking, we must also think about the means by which we will achieve those goals.

If rewards in an afterlife were our only purpose in performing right actions, it would be possible to believe that right actions might be adequate, in and of themselves alone, to achieve this goal. But if our purpose is to build a relationship with God and become all God wants us to be, then we must ask whether performing right actions is sufficient, in and of itself alone, to achieve this purpose.

Doing Right Things

Most certainly, doing right things and avoiding wrong ones is an essential part of growing to become all we are capable of being. We do not grow by doing things that harm other people or our own true good, even if we do them in good faith. E.g:

Imagine that, in the midst of a powerful history of communal or tribal hatreds, a certain person makes the decision that he should take part in the massacre of his perceived enemies and does so. In the words of the Second Vatican Council, I would be compelled to say that his very dignity lies in following his conscience, even when he is wrong. Despite this, I would have to add that his decision has hurt him. He has become a murderer, and for the rest of his life, whenever he looks in a mirror, that is what he will see. To make serious progress as a human being, he would need to recognise that his decision had been a morally wrong one, and he would need to do all he could to repair the damage he had caused.

Taking Responsibility for our Actions

Doing right things is, however, no more than a means to an end and it is not capable, in and of itself alone, of achieving the end. Morality is about growth as moral persons and for growth more is required than simply performing right actions, as the following examples will show.

As children grow, it is important that they learn right habits, but it is also important that they gradually learn to take responsibility for their own actions. If they learn wrong habits from their parents, or if they rebel against their parents and adopt wrong habits themselves, they will encounter problems. But if they do not learn to take responsibility for their own actions, obedience to parents will gradually become an obstacle rather than a help to their true growth as persons. A forty-year-old who cannot take responsibility, but must in all things still follow parents, is not an ideal for anyone. If this is true in all aspects of life, it is true also of moral life.

Years ago much marriage counselling was directive, that is, a couple presented their problem to the counsellor and the counsellor responded by indicating the best way to resolve the problem. All too often, however, the couple went away not fully convinced the solution would work—or even not wanting it to work—and tried the solution in a half-hearted way; when it consequently did not work, they blamed the counsellor. So counselling became non-directive, that is, the counsellor undertook the harder task of helping the couple to find their own solution to the problem, a solution they were both convinced of and committed to. Even if the solution the couple decided on was not the one the counsellor thought ideal, it was the best solution in the circumstances because the couple took responsibility for it.

Imagine that a person is faced with a moral choice, but it is a choice between two morally good things, with neither option involving a moral offence or harm to other persons. The person takes the matter seriously and goes through a very careful process of conscience, eventually choosing Option A. From heaven, five scholars and six saints have observed the process and agree that Option B would have been better. Granted that no moral offence or harm to others is involved, it may still be argued that the careful process of conscience and taking responsibility makes Option A better for this person, for it is the whole process, and in a particular way the taking of personal responsibility, that brings about the moral growth and goodness of the person.

There are persons who, because of fear or laziness, do not want to take personal responsibility for moral choices. They want either the Bible or Church authority or a charismatic leader or popular opinion or a peer group to take the responsibility for them, so that all that will be left to them is to follow this authority. This cannot be called 'the very dignity' of these persons, for they have not truly taken personal responsibility for their decisions and will not grow as they should. Mere obedience, to either religious authority or popular opinion, is not 'the very dignity' of a person.

Many moral decisions are easy, so it is easy to take responsibility for them. The more difficult the matter we are dealing with, the more difficult it will be to make the decision and take responsibility for it. But it is also true that, the more difficult the issue, the more we will grow through the process of taking true responsibility for our actions.

This need for personal responsibility is fully in agreement with Catholic teaching.

- 'By free will one shapes one's own life. Human freedom is a force for growth and maturity in truth and goodness.'[15]
- 'Freedom makes us responsible for our acts to the extent that they are voluntary.'[16]
- 'The right to the exercise of freedom, especially in moral and religious matters, is an inalienable requirement of the dignity of the human person.'[17]
- 'Conscience enables one to assume responsibility for the acts performed.'[18]

Thus it is important that we take personal responsibility for our decisions and it is also important that we get them right. We will not grow unless we take personal responsibility for our actions. But, even if we do take personal responsibility, we will still not grow if our decisions harm other people or our own true good; for growth, both of these elements are essential. Any adequate understanding of the meaning of the word 'morality' must, therefore, contain both elements.

---

[15] Catechism of the Catholic Church, no.1731.

[16] ibid. no.1734.

[17] ibid. no.1738.

[18] ibid. no.1781.

MORAL CHOICES

Many times each day we make choices between right and wrong. Most of these choices are minor, though major choices sometimes present themselves. Through these choices we take responsibility for each of our actions. Then, through the sum total of all these choices, big and small, we gradually and imperceptibly begin to take personal responsibility for the moral direction of our entire lives and to determine our moral identity. Over a long period of time we gradually determine whether we are basically just or unjust persons, kind or unkind, truthful or untruthful, honest or dishonest, loving or selfish. We determine at which of the six levels of morality mentioned earlier we habitually act.

Virtues and Vices

Most of the actions we perform each day are the result of moral choices we made long ago and of the habits that were formed as a result of those choices, so that we do not need to think about the morality of the action each time we perform it. There are, of course, right habits and wrong habits. Rights habits are called virtues and wrong habits are called vices. A person possessing the virtue of justice will, from long practice, instinctively react justly in every new situation. A person possessing the vice of injustice will, from equally long practice, instinctively seek an advantage over others without caring whether they might be hurt. A truly moral person is one who has worked so hard and long at forming good habits (virtues) that things such as justice, love, compassion, truth, honesty and integrity are a natural part of that person's instinctive reaction to any new situation that presents itself.

The hardest moral struggle occurs when we have deliberately chosen something wrong in the past and must now fight against the wrong habits that have been formed, e.g. if we have constantly told lies or spread gossip or been dishonest.

Experienced policemen would say that for almost all people a first murder is an overwhelming experience, but that if the same person goes on to commit further murders, even murder can become easy: that is, a habit or vice. In any particular field, whether it be murder or stealing or anything else, the first sin is the hardest one to commit; after that, the sin becomes easier to commit and the habit becomes more and more entrenched.

There are times when we must struggle against habits even when the habit has involved no deliberate wrongdoing on our part. This happens whenever in our upbringing our elders transmitted to us habits of thinking and acting that we later came to realise were morally wrong. Among these unjust attitudes that we may have innocently inherited are those of:

- men towards women
- white people towards people of a different colour
- Christians towards Jews and Muslims
- people born in a country towards immigrant peoples

- people of richer countries towards those of poorer countries
- people of today towards people of the past through a sense of pride and superiority, or towards people of the future through destruction of the environment.

At times we can be forced to reassess our most simple actions. For example, we long ago accepted that it is morally right to eat with a knife and fork and we have done this all our lives without a single further thought about its morality. But what about all the disposable utensils (and packaging) that are thrown away each day, including disposable knives and forks? Can the thought of all this waste of limited resources cause us to think again?

The Basic Choice (the 'Fundamental Option')

Through many choices between right and wrong we gradually and imperceptibly form our moral identity. In this process we can then find that in our inmost core we have made a choice, not just between right and wrong, but also between goodness and badness. Note:

> For the sake of clarity I prefer to use the terms 'good' and 'bad' of persons and the terms 'right' and 'wrong' of thoughts and actions. As I shall use the terms, persons are good or bad (that is, this is the choice they have made in their inmost core), while thoughts and actions are right or wrong (that is, their particular thoughts and actions can be right or wrong).
>
> Much of Catholic morality comes originally from the Latin language and there the word *malum* means both 'wrong' and

'bad', while the word *bonum* means both 'right' and 'good'. Thus the distinction between good and bad on the one hand, and right and wrong on the other, has no real history behind it, and this should be kept in mind in reading any books on Catholic morality.

Furthermore, the word *malum* is all too frequently translated into English as 'evil' and this word is too easily applied to many actions. In most cases all the Latin text meant to say was that a certain action is wrong, and it is misleading to translate it as 'bad', let alone as 'evil'. 'Evil' is a powerful English word and it should not be used lightly. In particular, the Latin phrase *intrinsice malum* should not be translated as 'intrinsically evil', but as 'in itself wrong'.

The choice between goodness and badness is not simply one more choice, even if at a deeper level than the other choices. It is rather a self-awareness of who we have come to be. We ought to spend time making it conscious and explicit in our lives but, because it is a self-awareness rather than a simple choice, it will never be possible to analyse it completely.

Of course, no human being is ever entirely good or entirely bad. A good person can do wrong things and a bad person can do right and even loving things. A good person can have certain vices and a bad person can have certain virtues. A bad person can become a good one and a good person can become a bad one. The basic choice between goodness and badness is always in process, never fully determined once and for all. In a famous sentence, St.

Augustine once prayed, 'Lord, make me pure, but not yet.' Did this make him good, bad or on the way?

At the same time, there is an intimate connection between the persons we are and the actions we perform. We attain goodness by doing right things and taking responsibility for them, but we will do right things only if we are seeking goodness. First comes the desire for goodness, then the choice of right actions as an expression of this desire. The right actions then reinforce the desire for goodness, turning it into a more powerful and constant striving. This in turn produces more right actions, and so the process continues. The essential starting point is the desire for goodness, for without this the process cannot even begin.

In any moral dilemma we can ask one of two questions: 'What is the right thing to do here?' or 'Where is goodness to be found here?' The two questions are actually one and the same question, but the second form of the question—seeking where goodness is to be found—is the more important form, for it better expresses the nature of morality as a relationship between ourselves, other people and God. Also, we can often be in doubt concerning the right thing to do, and the seeking of goodness can sometimes be a surer guide.

Mortal Sin

Within this context, a word needs to be added on the ideas of mortal sin and hell, for false ideas on these subjects can cripple our understanding of morality.

The word 'mortal' means 'death-dealing', so I suggest that a mortal sin must be something that is truly death-dealing. To have this effect, it must in some manner touch the inmost core of a person's being, it must be something so fundamental that it changes the moral identity of a person and makes a good person a bad person. The action must in some manner involve the denial of a relationship with God or at least the exclusion of the influence of God over the action one is contemplating ('You don't exist or, if you do, I reject you as a guide for my thinking and acting in this matter'). Even a single action can turn a formerly good person into a bad one, and we have all heard of examples of such things as murder, rape, sexual abuse of minors or ethnic cleansing that would fit into this category. The change from good to bad can also happen more gradually, as the following case will show:

A lawyer faithfully observes the rules of his profession for twenty years. Then one day he sees an investment that will almost certainly bring a rapid profit. Feeling very guilty, he takes a modest amount of money from trust funds he manages for clients and invests it. It brings a rapid profit and he instantly repays the money, feeling very relieved. But he also can't help thinking that, if he had only taken a larger amount of money, he would have made a greater profit. He has committed the first sin, and a second and third will be easier and the amounts will be larger until, somewhere along this road, he has ceased to be a good person and become a bad one.

I suggest that a sin that is not death-dealing, that does not change someone from a good person to a bad person, should not be given the name 'mortal'.

On this point I find the teaching of the Catholic Church ambiguous. The encyclical *Veritatis Splendor* says that 'mortal sin is sin whose object is grave matter' and it specifically adds that: '…care will have to be taken not to reduce mortal sin to an act of 'fundamental option'. For mortal sin exists also when a person knowingly and willingly, for whatever reason, chooses something gravely disordered.' (no.70)

This appears to say that the free and willing choice of grave matter is a mortal sin, even when it does not affect the fundamental option. The encyclical, however, goes on to say that: 'In fact, such a choice already includes contempt for the divine law, a rejection of God's love for humanity and the whole of creation.'

This statement, on the other hand, appears to come very close to saying that every free choice of grave matter does affect the fundamental option. Surely the answer depends on what we understand by 'grave matter'.

I suggest that the ambiguity occurs because there have been far too many cases in Catholic morality of the currency of mortal sin being devalued. For example, it is quite misleading and harmful to moral life to speak of mortal sin in relation to things such as a person missing Sunday Mass once or having a 'bad thought' about something sexual, or a priest forgetting to say night prayer from the breviary. It is ludicrous to say that such actions necessarily involve 'contempt for the divine law, a rejection of God's love for humanity and the whole of creation.' It is wrong and harmful to present the moral life as walking through a minefield of mortal sins which are likely to explode at any minute. It is vitally important that this type of thinking be left behind, for this devaluing of the currency of mortal sin has caused innumerable problems and misunderstandings in Catholic morality. It seems that they all came from the attempt to coerce people to do things they might otherwise not have wished to do (e.g. go to Mass every Sunday, not desire sex outside marriage, and pray the entire Divine Office each day), and it has caused immense harm in the moral understanding of Catholic people.

I suggest that we are on far safer ground, and have a much better basis on which to build the whole of morality, if we restrict our understanding of mortal sin to those things that truly change a person from a good person to a bad person.

These ideas should not lead us to the opposite extreme of believing that mortal sin is something remote that could never happen to us. We are all capable of a death-dealing sin. We all know that, unless we refuse to allow it to happen, we are capable of great hatred and of the actions that can flow from it. We can all crash back to the level of Lamech at any moment. It can also be said that mortal sin lies at the end of a path, and in order to avoid it, it is better not to take the first step along that path.

We must also be careful not to fall into the mentality of Rycker and think that, as long as we do not perform a mortal or death-dealing action, everything is in its place.

Any attempt to say that a particular action is 'only' a venial sin is to fall straight into the mentality of Rycker. We must remember that the only sure way to avoid a death-dealing relationship is to have a life-giving or loving relationship.

There is a corollary to all that has just been said, namely, that forgiveness of mortal sin requires a profound conversion, for it must be as life-giving as the sin was death-dealing.

Perhaps the whole matter can be summed up by saying that, at the end of our lives, God is not likely to ask us only whether we have truly repented since we last committed what was considered to be a mortal sin. God is more likely to say to us: 'Welcome, please come in. We have all the time in the world, so take your time and tell me your whole story. You have had 'x' amount of living years. What have you done with that time? In what ways is the world a better place because you have lived in it? In what ways are the lives of other people better for having known you? What sort of person have you made of yourself? At this supreme moment of your life, tell me, who are you?'

We will know that we are in the presence of a loving God, so we will not be afraid and will speak freely. However, we will also know that we cannot deceive God and must not deceive ourselves.

HEAVEN AND HELL

Moral monsters have existed in every century and it is easy to think of several famous ones in our own lifetime. The lives of some have been so shocking that it appears that badness can exist at the inmost core of a person and that people can die in this badness. So, does hell exist? On the other hand, could a God of infinite love really create a state of eternal torment?

In answering this question, it is wise to be careful of the language that is used. In the Gospel of Mark, Jesus is reported as saying: 'If your hand causes you to stumble, cut it off. It is better for you to enter life maimed than to have two hands and go to hell, to the unquenchable fire.'[19] It does not make sense to say that the first half of this sentence must not be taken literally ('cut it off'), but the second half must be taken literally ('unquenchable fire'). The language of the whole sentence must be seen as figurative and we must accept our profound ignorance on the subject of what hell might be like. We must firmly put aside all ideas of burning lakes of sulphur, devils, pitchforks etc. etc., for these cannot be anything more than figurative language invented by human beings. All we can really say is that heaven is the presence of God and hell is the absence of God.

I believe that God has an absolute respect for human free will, so I believe that those who explicitly do not want God's presence after their death will not have this presence imposed on them. If it is understood in this sense—as the individual's free choice for God's absence—I believe we must admit that something or other that could be called 'hell' exists. Committing a truly mortal sin, in the sense in which I have understood that term, is such a choice.

---

[19] Mark 9:43.

What happens to such people, however, is quite beyond our knowledge. My personal belief is that there could never be a time, in this world or any other, when God would cease to love all people or to long for their growth towards goodness. I believe this is particularly true for all those who sincerely came to the belief that there is no God because of the evil and suffering around them or the bad example of religious people. In saying this, I would seem to be in good company:

> For I am convinced that neither death, nor life, nor angels, nor rulers, nor things present, nor things to come, nor powers, nor height, nor depth, nor anything else in all creation, will be able to separate us from the love of God in Christ Jesus our Lord.[20]

Much preaching on hell over the centuries has been grossly overzealous, seriously devaluing the currency of mortal sin, in an attempt to induce fear in people and coerce them to make the decisions the preacher thought they should make. I do not believe that Jesus did this, but he frequently presented moral dilemmas in the starkest possible terms. One moral decision on a trivial matter may not seem to be of great moment, but it is the sum total of all our decisions that creates our very moral identity in our inmost core, and Jesus would insist in strong and even exaggerated language that this is all-important.

---

[20] Rom. 8:38–39.

AN ASSESSMENT

The Catholic Church has at times been like a rock standing against a powerful flood of popular trends. It has at times been a lone voice asking some of the questions that have needed to be asked. It has been prepared to be reviled in order to stand up for things it believes are truly important for the good of all people. It has shown a good and right concern that people should do the right thing, because it knows that doing wrong things is not the way of moral growth. It has striven hard to base morality on objective principles rather than on subjective thoughts and feelings. It has devoted much energy toward the manner of determining right and wrong actions, and many principles have been evolved over the centuries that are of enduring value.

At the same time, Rycker was not entirely to blame for his attitudes, for he had listened well to many things said to him in church, school and seminary. Among the major weaknesses in the Church's practice are the following:

- Because of an emphasis on right and wrong actions, there has been the tendency to place at the centre of morality the following of moral rules rather than the building of relationships.
- There has been too much of the attitude of 'getting into heaven by avoiding wrong actions', and the predominant motivation has too often been fear of an angry god.
- There has been the consequent tendency to stress the doing of right actions in and of themselves, and

to downplay the importance of the individual taking personal responsibility for each action. This has not assisted moral growth and maturity.

- In determining what was the right thing to do, the strong emphasis was on doing what Church authorities said one should do. It must be said that the teaching authority within the Catholic Church has not always respected the role of conscience; it has sometimes seen conscience as the enemy of authority rather than its essential ally.

- Because of the intensity of the desire of authorities that people should do right things, there has been an all-too-frequent devaluing of the currency of mortal sin, seeking to coerce right actions in minor matters, and significantly increasing the load of guilt Catholic people carried.

- Because the Bible does not give us clear and simple guidelines concerning right actions, it has not been given a sufficiently important place as a source of moral thinking.

- The natural moral law as a source of moral thinking has been taken too far. This is particularly true in relation to sexual morality, where a restricted and mechanical view of what is 'according to nature' has come to dominate. This tendency has been taken so far that the entire concept of natural law has at times come into disrepute and now needs to be rescued.

- Rather than look to improve the reasoning it has used

in its documents, Church authority has often done no more than insist repeatedly on the authority of the person issuing the document.

- In all of this, the teaching authority in the Church has relied too heavily on the wisdom and moral sense of a few people in the Vatican and has been lacking in its efforts to make its moral statements reflect a true consensus within the whole Church, or even within the bishops of the Church. It has not known how to value and make use of dissenting opinions, despite their sincerity.

Church authority has had a fear that any weakening in its stance would lead to an irresistible flood of people doing whatever they wanted to do, so it has relied too much on authority and too little on reason, and because of this it has lost much of its credibility. There is a profound conviction in the minds of many people that the teaching authority has been wrong on certain key subjects in the areas of power and sex, and this has also profoundly weakened its credibility. The sad irony is that this loss of credibility has contributed to some of the very things the teaching authority has most feared.

So where should Church authority go from here? We may perhaps answer this question by contrasting the Bible and Church authority. The story of the Bible is that of the people of Israel struggling to know what was the right thing to do despite a lack of clear divine directions. Struggling to determine the right thing to do and actually doing it were both seen as essential elements of that story. It was by this combination that people grew in moral stature and, as a broad plan, it came from God. Church authority, on the other hand, has frequently sought to spell out in detail the right thing to do in every circumstance, so that morality was then reduced to doing what Church authority had told us was right. In briefest summary, God always treated people as adults, while the Church has too often treated them as children.

MORAL IMMATURITY

The defects in moral teaching that I have highlighted run the serious risk of producing morally immature human beings. I believe that this has been a common feature in sexual offenders, contributing to the quite distorted moral thinking that is so prevalent among them ('I'm only showing these boys how to love', 'God made me the way I am, so He must have wanted me to act this way'). There needs to be a concerted effort to bring about healthier and more mature moral thinking.

CHAPTER THREE

SEXUAL MORALITY

The constantly repeated argument of the Catholic Church is that God created human sex for two reasons: as a means of expressing and fostering love between a couple (the unitive aspect) and as the means by which new human life is brought into being (the procreative aspect). The argument then says that the use of sex is 'according to nature' only when it serves both of these God-given purposes, and that both are truly present only within marriage, and even then only when intercourse is open to new life, so that all other use of the sexual faculties is morally wrong.[21]

I have no problem with the idea that human sex has both a unitive and a procreative aspect, but I have four basic difficulties with the teaching that every single act of

---

[21] The most important papal document on sexual morality of the last century, the encyclical letter *Humanae Vitae*, expressed the argument thus: 'Such teaching, many times set forth by the teaching office of the church, is founded on the unbreakable connection, which God established and which men and women may not break of their own initiative, between the two meanings of the conjugal act: the unitive meaning and the procreative meaning. Indeed, in its intimate nature, the conjugal act, while it unites the spouses in a most profound bond, also places them in a position (*idoneos facit*) to generate new life, according to laws inscribed in the very being of man and woman. By protecting both of these essential aspects, the unitive and the procreative, the conjugal act preserves in an integral manner the sense of mutual and true love and its ordering to the exalted vocation of human beings to parenthood.' Pope Paul VI, encyclical letter *Humanae Vitae*, 26th July 1968, no.12.

intercourse must contain both of these aspects.

A SIN AGAINST GOD

The first difficulty is that through this teaching the Church is saying that the essence of sexual sin is that it is a direct offence against God because it is a violation of what is claimed to be the divine and natural order that God established. It is claimed that God inserted into nature itself the demand that every human sexual act be both unitive and procreative. If it does not contain both of these elements, it is against 'nature' as established by God. This raises two serious questions, one concerning nature and the other concerning God.

The Question Concerning Nature

In relation to nature, may we not argue that, if this divine and natural order exists in relation to our sexual faculties, it should exist in many other areas of human life as well? So should not the Church's arguments concerning sex point to many other fields where God has given a divine purpose to some created thing, such that it would be a sin against God to use that thing in any other way? Why is it that it is only in relation to sex that this claim is made? I remember reading years ago the mocking argument that the natural God-given purpose of human eyes is to look forwards (and that is why God placed them on the front of our heads), so rear vision mirrors in cars are against nature and, therefore, immoral. Granting that this is a mocking argument, does it not raise questions about what we mean by 'nature' and 'natural', and how difficult it is to draw moral consequences from a claim to a divinely established nature?

The Question Concerning God

Imagine that you read in the newspaper two stories of Australians being physically attacked while overseas. Imagine that the first concerns a man who has largely brought it on himself by drinking too much and getting into a fight, while the other concerns a woman who has not been drinking, has done nothing to provoke anyone and whose name is Julia Gillard. The second story would be by far the bigger, with profuse apologies from the government of that nation. The reason would be that, as Prime Minister of Australia, she represents this country, and an unprovoked attack on her is an attack on the nation. We would all agree that this story concerns a far greater offence. In the same way, a physical attack on Queen Elizabeth would have the entire United Kingdom up in arms.

This helps us to understand the argument in past centuries that striking a king was far more serious than striking a commoner. In line with this, it was said, the greatest king by far is God, and so an offence against God is far more serious than any offence against a mere human being.

Because all sexual sins were seen as direct offences against God, they were, therefore, all seen as most serious sins. This put all sexual sins right up there with the other sin that is directly against God, blasphemy, and this helps to explain why, in the Catholic Church, sexual morality has long been given exaggerated importance.

For centuries the Church has taught that every sexual sin is a mortal sin.[22] In this field, it was held, there are no venial sins. According to this teaching, even deliberately deriving pleasure from thinking about sex with anyone other than one's spouse, no matter how briefly, is a mortal sin. The teaching may not be proclaimed aloud today as much as before, but it was proclaimed by many Popes,[23] it has never been retracted and it has affected countless people.

This teaching fostered belief in an incredibly angry god, for this god would condemn a person to an eternity in hell for a single unrepented moment of deliberate pleasure arising from sexual desire. I simply do not believe in such a god. Indeed, I positively reject such a god.

My first rebellion against Church teaching on sex came, therefore, not directly from a rejection of what the Church said about sex, but a rejection of the god that this teaching presented.

The parable of the prodigal son may help us here.[24] The younger son had received the entire share of the property that would come to him and he had wasted it. He had no

---

[22] See Noldin-Schmitt, *Summa Theologiae Moralis*, Feliciani Rauch, Innsbruck, 1960 Vol.I, Supplement De Castitate, p.17, no.2; Aertnys-Damen, Theologia Moralis, Marietti, Rome, 1956, vol.1, no.599, p.575. The technical term constantly repeated was *mortale ex toto genere suo*. The sin of taking pleasure from thinking about sex was called *delectatio morose*.

[23] For example, Clement VII (1592–1605) and Paul V (1605–1621) said that those who denied this teaching should be denounced to the Inquisition.

[24] Luke 15:11–32.

right to one further square centimetre of the property, for the entire remaining property would now go by strict right to the elder son ('You are with me always and all I have is yours' v.31). The father respected his elder son's rights and would take nothing from him. When, however, it came to the hurt the prodigal son had caused to his father by abandoning him and wasting the property he had worked so hard for, the father brushed this aside out of love for his son and insisted that he be welcomed and treated as a son rather than a servant. The message is surely that God cares about the rights of human beings and what they do to one another, but is big enough, loving enough and forgiving enough not to get angry at direct offences against God.

When a person takes great offence at even a trivial remark, we tend to speak of that person as a 'little' person, while a person who can shrug off most negative comments is a 'big' person. My reading of the Bible leads me to believe in a very big God indeed who is not easily offended by direct offences. I believe, for instance, that God shrugs off much of what is called 'blasphemy' as an understandable human reaction to the felt injustice of evil and suffering in this world. I do not believe that God is in the least offended when parents who have just lost a child rage in terrible anger against God.

In this vein, I must ask whether God will be offended by any sexual thought or action considered solely as an offence against an order established by God, before any question of its effect on other persons, oneself or the community is taken into account.

It must be added that, in the response to revelations of sexual abuse, the idea of every sexual sin as a direct mortal sin against God became a most serious problem, for far too many Church authorities saw the offence primarily in terms of a sexual offence against God. This sexual sin was seen as the great mortal sin, far more serious than what was seen as the lesser sin committed against the minor.

At the same time, sexual sins were seen as sins of weakness rather than malice, so forgiveness was always easily given. The sexual mortal sin involved in paedophilia was, therefore, to be treated according to the criteria governing all sexual offences: repentance, confession, absolution, total forgiveness by God and hence restoration to the status quo. This contributed greatly to the practice of moving offenders from one parish to another in the name of Christian forgiveness. There was never going to be an adequate response to abuse as long as many people thought primarily in terms of sexual offences against God rather than harm caused to the victims.

PROVEN FACT OR SIMPLE ASSERTION?

My second objection to the teaching is that it appears to be a mere assertion rather than a proven fact.

No one disputes the facts that sexual intercourse is the normal means of creating new life and that it can and ought to be a powerful force in helping couples to express and strengthen their love. Both the unitive and procreative elements are, therefore, foundational aspects of marriage as an institution of the whole human race.

But are they essential elements of each individual marriage, no matter what the circumstances? For example, if a couple are told by medical experts that any child they had would suffer from a serious and crippling hereditary illness, are they going against God's will if they decide to adopt rather than have children of their own? Beyond this, are the unitive and procreative elements essential in every single act of sexual intercourse; and, if so, on what basis?

There are always problems when human beings claim that they know the mind of God. So is the statement that it is God's will, and indeed order, that both the unitive and procreative aspects must necessarily be present in each act of sexual intercourse a proven fact or a simple assertion? If it is claimed to be a proven fact, what are the proofs? Why do Church documents not present such proofs?[25] Would not any proofs have to include the experience of millions of people in the very human endeavour of seeking to combine sex, love and the procreation of new life in the midst of the turbulence of human sexuality and the complexities of human life?

If it is only an assertion, is there any reason why we should not apply the principle of logic: what is freely asserted may be freely denied? If it is no more than an

---

[25] In recent years there has been an appeal to anthropology, but I have not seen a clear statement of how anthropology demands that every act of intercourse include both the unitive and procreative purpose.

assertion, does it really matter who it is who makes the assertion or how often it is made? Where are the arguments in favour of the assertion that would convince an open and honest conscience?

CONCENTRATION ON THE PHYSICAL

The third objection is that the teaching of the Catholic Church is to far too great an extent based on a consideration of what is seen as the God-given nature of the physical acts in themselves, rather than on how such acts affect persons and relationships. Moral questions are then concerned solely with the details and circumstances of the physical acts rather than of the persons performing them. And the Church continues to do this at a time when the whole trend in moral theology is in the opposite direction.

As a result it gets into impossible difficulties in analysing physical acts without a context of human relations. For example, some married couples find that there is a blockage preventing the sperm from reaching the ovum, but that in a simple procedure a doctor can take the husband's sperm and insert it into the wife in such a way that it passes the blockage and enables conception. But the Vatican condemned this action because the physical act was not considered 'integral'.

TEACHING OF JESUS

The fourth objection is that the entire idea of the necessity for both the unitive and procreative element in each act of intercourse is not based on anything Jesus said or implied, but comes from ideas outside the Bible concerning acts that are said to be natural and acts that are said to be against nature. Sex is a powerful force in human life. In seeking to understand its moral nature, why would the Church not turn to anything Jesus said or did and instead rely on ideas from other sources?

HIERARCHICAL TEACHING AND CATHOLIC PRACTICE

We are left with the fact that the Catholic Church is propounding a teaching that only a minority of Catholics still accept, especially among the young. Western society as a whole has rejected this teaching and gone toward a position that is in many ways an opposite extreme. Few people, it seems, are left to argue for a middle ground between the two. It is this middle ground that I now wish to explore.

THE MIDDLE GROUND

If we decide to leave behind an ethic that sees sex in terms of a direct offence against God, that emphasises individual physical acts rather than persons and relationships, and that is based on a repeated assertion rather than an argument, where should we go? I suggest that the answer is that we should move to an ethic that: firstly, sees any offence against God as being brought about not by the sexual act in itself, but by the harm caused to human beings; secondly, speaks in terms of persons and relationships rather than physical acts; thirdly, looks to the Gospels and the person of Jesus for its inspiration; and then, fourthly, builds an argument on these three foundations rather than on unproven assertions.

Harm to Persons

If it is impossible to sustain an entire sexual ethic on the basis of direct offences against God, all the evidence tells us that God cares greatly about human beings and takes a very serious view of any harm done to them, through sexual desire or any other cause. As the Gospel of Mark says:

> If any of you put a stumbling block before one of these little ones who believe in me, it would be better for you if a great millstone were hung around your neck and you were thrown into the sea.[26]

Even given the deliberate Semitic exaggeration in these words, does not this quotation alone tell us what God thinks of paedophilia? Does it not also tell us that Jesus puts the emphasis on the harm done to the victim rather than on some direct offence against God?

---

[26] Mark 9:42.

Or take the quotation from Matthew's Gospel:

Then they will answer, "Lord, when was it that we saw you hungry or thirsty or a stranger or naked or sick or in prison, and did not take care of you?" Then he will answer them, "Truly I tell you, just as you did not do it to one of the least of these, you did not do it to me."[27]

In these two quotations, Jesus identifies with the weakest persons in the community, and tells us that any harm done to them is a harm done to himself. I suggest, therefore, that we should look at sexual morality in terms of the good or harm done to persons and the relationships between them rather than in terms of a direct offence against God.

Following from this, may we say that sexual pleasure, like all other pleasure, is in itself morally neutral, neither right nor wrong? Is it rather the circumstances affecting persons and relationships that make this pleasure right or wrong, e.g. a right pleasure for a married couple seeking reconciliation after a disagreement, a wrong pleasure for a man committing rape?

The Church vs. Modern Western Society

To take this further, if we go beneath the particular teachings of the Catholic Church on sex and come to its most foundational beliefs, I suggest that there is a fundamental point on which the Church and modern Western society

---

[27] Matt. 25:44–45.

57

appear to be moving in opposite directions. The Church is saying that love is the very deepest longing of the human heart and sex is one of the most important expressions of love that we have, so people should do all in their power to ensure that sex retains its ability to express love as deeply as possible. They should, therefore, make sure that sex does not become so trivialised—for themselves individually or for the community as a whole—that it loses its power to express this deepest love. Modern Western society, on the other hand, has become more and more accepting of casual sexual activity that is not related to love or relationship.

In its simplest terms, the Church is saying that, because love is all-important and because sex is so vital a way of expressing love, sex is always serious; while modern society appears to be saying more and more that sex is 'a bit of fun' and not in itself serious.

On this basic point I find myself instinctively more in sympathy with the views of the Church than with those of modern society. It was, in fact, the effects of sexual abuse on minors more than anything else that convinced me that sex is always serious.

Do not Harm vs. Love your Neighbour

Because I see sex as serious, I do not simply conclude that all sex is good as long as it does not harm anyone. I would never want to put the matter in those simple terms, for I have seen far too much harm caused by this attitude.

The idea is expressed in negative terms ('Do not harm') and inevitably contains within itself the serious risk of brinkmanship; that is, that, with little thought for the good of the other person involved, one may seek one's own pleasure and, in doing so, go right up to the very brink of causing harm to another. In a field as turbulent as this, it is inevitable that many people utilising such a principle will go over that brink.

Jesus invariably said 'Love your neighbour' and this implies more than the negative desire to not harm. It implies genuine respect for the other and positively wanting and seeking the good of the other. The essential difference between the two is that an attitude of 'Do no harm' can put oneself first, while 'Love your neighbour' must put the other first. A Christian ethic must, at the very least, be expressed in these positive terms. It is only on this positive basis of respecting and seeking the good of the other that we could feel confident of having found a truly Christian ethic. We could never have that confidence on the basis of the negative principle of 'Do no harm'.

In doing this, we must take the harm that can be caused by sexual desire very seriously indeed, and look carefully at the circumstances that can make morally wrong the seeking of sexual pleasure because they involve harm to others, to oneself or to the community. Some of these factors are: physical or psychological violence, deceit and self-deceit, harming a third person (e.g. a spouse), using another person for one's own gratification, treating people as sexual objects rather than as persons, separating sex from love to the extent that sex loses its ability to express the depths of love, trivialising sex so that it loses its seriousness, allowing the desire for present satisfaction to restrict the ability to respond to the deeper longings of the human heart, harming the possibility of permanent commitment, failing to respect the connection that exists between sex and new life, failing to respect the need to build a relationship patiently and carefully, and failing to respect the common good of the whole community.

It can be seen from the above that I have serious difficulties with the idea that 'anything goes.' In reacting against one extreme, there is always the danger of going to the opposite extreme. I believe that this is what many people have done in relation to sex.

THE TEACHING OF JESUS

The major criterion of sexual morality that Jesus gave us was his universal principle of 'love your neighbour'. He presented this principle as the basis of everything in Christian life and this means that, like any other act in a Christian's life, a sexual act should be based on a genuine desire for all that is good for the other person rather than simply on self-interest. Since we may assume that he was not naïve about either the good or the harm that sexual desire can cause, we must conclude that, having said this, he believed he had said all that needed to be said. In this the Church has definitely not followed his example.

THE CENTRAL QUESTIONS

I therefore suggest that the central questions concerning sexual morality are:

- Are we moving towards a genuinely Christian ethic if we base all our sexual thoughts and actions on a profound respect for the relationships that give meaning, purpose and direction to human life, and on loving our neighbour as we would want our neighbour to love us?

- Within this context, may we ask whether a sexual act is morally right when positively: it is based on a genuine love of neighbour, that is, a genuine desire for what is good for the other person involved rather than solely on self-interest, and negatively: there are no damaging elements such as harm to a third person, any form of coercion or deceit, or any harm to the ability of sex to express love?

- Is the question of when these circumstances might apply—and whether and to what extent they might apply both inside and outside marriage—a question for discussion and debate by both the Church community and the wider community, and then a decision (and the taking of responsibility) before God, other people, and one's own deeper self by each individual?

CONCLUSION

Many would object that what I have proposed would not give clear and simple rules to people; but God never promised us that everything in the moral life would be clear and simple. Morality is not just about doing right things; it is also about struggling to know what is the right thing to do.

Many would also object that such ideas would be too easily abused and would lead to people doing whatever they wanted to. Yes, these ideas would be abused, for sexual desire is a most powerful force, and for that very reason any moral framework on the subject will be abused, just as Catholic teaching has been abused and ignored. But morality is not just about doing what everyone else around us is doing; it is about taking a genuine personal responsibility for everything we do. And sexual morality is about being profoundly sensitive to the needs and vulnerabilities of the people with whom we interact. It is through this sensitivity that we will grow as moral persons, in a way that mere obedience to authority can never achieve.

I believe that there is normally a far better chance of a sexual act meeting the requirements I have suggested within a permanent and vowed relationship than there is outside such a relationship. But I could not draw the simple conclusion that: inside a vowed relationship everything is good, outside everything is bad. The complexities of human nature and the turbulence of sexuality do not allow for such simple answers. Ultimately, we must come to a sense of personal responsibility, with all its difficulties and dangers, but also with all its potential for growth.

The encyclical *Humanae Vitae* of 1968 was a genuine watershed in the relationship between papal teaching and Catholic people, and I cannot see the slightest possibility of the Catholic people as a whole ever returning to the current hierarchical teaching on sexual morality. If the gap between the two is to be bridged, it must be on the basis of a mutual acceptance of a middle ground. I hope that I have pointed in fruitful directions.

The traditional teaching of the Catholic Church on sexual morality fostered belief in an incredibly angry god. And belief in such an angry god—specifically in the field of sex—has been a most significant contribution to the unhealthy culture I am seeking to describe in this book. It can lead to sexuality being seen as dark, secretive and troublesome.

Even at this early stage, I hope that we can see that a priest who still basically believes in an angry god, whose moral thinking is confused and immature, and who sees all sexual morality in terms of mortal sins directly against God, is living in an unhealthy culture, a culture out of which many different unhealthy actions can, and do, arise.

CHAPTER FOUR

THE MALE CHURCH

The sexual abuse of minors is overwhelmingly a male problem. Yes, some women have also offended, but the vast majority of offences have been by men.

Elizabeth Johnson speaks of a Church in which all power is in the hands of men, where all the dogmas, teachings, laws, customs and even attitudes are those of men. All authority is in the hands of men, and all the imagery is masculine; after all the talk, God is still fundamentally seen as male. Indeed, even men's ways of being human beings have been seen as normative for all human beings. Women have had no voice in articulating the Church's doctrine, morals or law. Banned from the pulpit and the altar, their wisdom has not been permitted to interpret the Gospels, nor their spirituality to lead the Church in prayer.[28]

David Ranson says that this absence of women from any positions of influence has led to many distortions in the Church. It has led to a serious underestimation of desire, imagination, dreaming and prophecy, and a failure to appreciate adequately the importance of such things as

---

[28] See Elizabeth A Johnson, *The Quest for the Living God*, Continuum, New York, 2007, ch.5, 'God Acting Womanish'.

sensitivity, touch, attentiveness, vulnerability, hospitality and compassion. These attitudes can take away the natural warmth and spontaneity of love and leave goodwill a vague term not directed at anyone or anything in particular. Simplicity can become confused with minimalism, self-mastery seen largely in terms of physical discipline, obedience equated with conformity and chastity reduced to control and lovelessness. The exclusion of the feminine, particularly in a celibate male culture, fosters a hermetically sealed culture in which there is an overdeveloped masculine ethos. In cultures built on a masculine energy that is not balanced by the feminine, there can be a growing incapacity for genuine interior reflection, an inability to relate with intimacy, a dependence on role and work for self-identification, and the loss of a humanising tenderness.[29]

Sandra Schneiders says that in looking at the Church, Christian feminists do not limit themselves to negative criticism, but have an alternative vision to present. This vision is characterised by equality, relatedness and empowerment rather than hierarchy, individualism and power. It seeks to restore to unity all those things that have been divided by a patriarchal mindset, e.g. spirit and body, transcendence and immanence, culture and nature, the rational and the intuitive, intelligence and emotion. It rejects stereotypes of both men and women and seeks to replace them with wholeness.[30]

---

[29] I am here indebted to an unpublished paper of David Ranson OCSA.

[30] Sandra M, Schneiders I.H.M., 'Feminist Spirituality', in *The New Dictionary of Catholic Spirituality*, Editor Michael Downey, The Liturgical Press, Collegeville, 1993, p. 395.

She points, for example, to the very male liturgy of the Mass, consisting as it does overwhelmingly of rational ideas poured out in a vast torrent of words over a largely passive congregation by a hierarchical and dominative priest. A liturgy that was a genuine combination of the male and female would be far richer.

For several years I held meetings of about eighty priests in the section of the Archdiocese of Sydney for which I had responsibility. Then I invited three female pastoral associates to attend the meetings and was struck by the way in which the presence of just three females among eighty men changed the whole tone of the meeting. Not all of the males appreciated the change at first, but I believe that most came to realise that the tone had become less abrasive, more positive and more co-operative than it had been.

A true equality between male and female in the Church would—by itself—change the entire culture dramatically. It is surely reasonable to assume that, if women had been given far greater importance and a much stronger voice, the Church would not have seen the same level of abuse and would have responded far better to this overwhelmingly male problem.

Furthermore, the temptation to subject all other matters to the overriding importance of one's own good name and honour, with the consequent hiding of anything that would bring shame, is also a largely a male concern, with a long history behind it in many so-called 'honour-shame' cultures. Through this, too, the absence of women has contributed both to abuse and to the poor response to abuse.

Rather than seek to develop these thoughts further, I want to give one example that will show how thoroughly the presence and voice of women is excluded and, ultimately, why women are excluded.

The Ordination of Women

By the middle decades of the twentieth century, the rising social and political claims of women for equality began also to affect most Christian denominations. The discussion of the ordination of women began in earnest ... There were nearly eight hundred articles and books written on this subject between 1960 and 2001, and interest in the subject does not seem to have waned since then.[31]

In 1994, Pope John Paul II wanted to put a stop to this increasing talk about the ordination of women to the priesthood, so he decided to publish a document that would have the maximum possible authority, and he knew that the support of the bishops of the world would assist in giving it greater authority. He prepared a document and then called to Rome the Presidents of the Bishops' Conferences from around the world. These Presidents were shown the document and then asked to endorse it in the name of all the bishops in their conferences.

---

[31] Gary Macy, *The Hidden History of Women's Ordination: Female Clergy in the Medieval West*, Oxford University Press, 2007, p. 10.

The Presidents replied that they could not do this, for they could not speak in the name of all the bishops without first asking them. They asked for two changes in the text of the document. They asked that the phrase '... having heard our brothers in the episcopal college...' be omitted, for the consultation with the Presidents alone did not add up to this. They also asked that the word 'irrevocable' be omitted.

(My account of these events comes from the verbal report given soon afterwards to the Australian bishops by its then Vice-President, Archbishop John Bathersby, who had attended the meeting in Rome.)

The document was published[32] with no reference to consultation with the bishops and with the word 'irrevocable' replaced by the words 'and that this judgement is to be definitively held by all the Church's faithful.'

My interpretation of these events is that Pope John Paul II wanted his document to have the maximum possible authority and so wanted the support of the bishops, but was unwilling to consult all of them because he could not guarantee their response. I believe that, had he asked them, the majority would have supported him, but a number wouldn't have. I do not know how large that number would have been, but the point is that neither did he, and he was unwilling to take the risk. I further believe that a significantly larger percentage of the bishops, probably a majority, would not have supported the use of words such

---

[32] John Paul II, Apostolic Letter, *Ordinatio Sacerdotalis*, 22 May 1994.

as 'irrevocable' or 'infallible', and this is surely indicated by the request of the Presidents that such words be omitted.

The dilemma for the Pope was that he could not publish his document with any hope that it would achieve the desired result of stopping even talk of the ordination of women if any noticeable number of bishops voted against it and a highly noticeable number, even a majority, did not want any reference to infallibility. How could a Pope claim the document was infallible—and should, therefore, stop all discussion—if Catholic women could reply: 'But a significant number of your own bishops don't agree with you, and most of them refuse to call the teaching infallible'?

Instead of consultation with the bishops, it was arranged that the Prefect of the Congregation for the Doctrine of the Faith, Cardinal Joseph Ratzinger, should in the following year publish a Response to a Doubt in which he said that:

> This teaching requires definitive assent, since, founded on
> the written Word of God, and from the beginning constantly
> preserved and applied in the Tradition of the Church, it
> has been set forth infallibly by the ordinary and universal
> Magisterium (cf. *Lumen Gentium*, 25).[33]

The use of the word 'infallible' here means that the Presidents of conferences were overruled and the word 'infallible' was used, so that John Paul II and, later, Ratzinger

---

[33] Congregation for the Doctrine of the Faith, 'Concerning the Teaching Contained in *Ordinatio Sacerdotalis, Responsum ad Dubium*', 28th October 1995.

himself (as Benedict XVI) could say that even talk of the ordination of women was forbidden.

The cardinal referred to two factors. The first is 'the written Word of God', which is presumably a reference to the fact that no women are recorded as being among those present at the Last Supper. The second is his appeal to the constant tradition of the Church over two thousand years. This is a particularly weak argument, for in appealing to the dead bishops of the past it pointedly excluded the living bishops of the present and, over the centuries, all too many of those past bishops had extreme negative views concerning women that today appal us.

There is an abundance of lurid statements to draw on. For example:

> I speak to you, O charmers of the clergy, appetizing flesh of the devil … you, poison of the minds, death of souls, venom of wine and eating, companions of the very stuff of sin, the cause of our ruin. You, I say, I exhort you women of the ancient enemy, you bitches, sows, screech-owls, night owls, she-wolves, blood suckers, who cry "Give, give without ceasing!"[34]

Today we would say that this writer has serious problems and is in urgent need of psychological help!

---

[34] Peter Damian, c.7 of *Contra Intemperantes Clericos* in PL145:410A–B, translation by Anne Llewellyn Barstow, *Married Priests and the Reforming Papacy: the Eleventh Century Debates*, Texts and Studies in Religion, 12, Edwin Mellon Press, New York, 1982. The text available to me is that of Gary Macy, *The Hidden History of Women's Ordination, Female Clergy in the Medieval West*, Oxford University Press, 2007, p. 113.

Rather than quote more of this type of statement, I prefer to add quotations from two sober canonists who were doing no more than quoting the reality of their times. Both acknowledge that for many centuries there had been women deacons, but Theodore Balsamon (12th century) then says, 'But the monthly affliction banished them from the divine and holy sanctuary.'[35] Matthew Blastares (14th century) says, 'They were forbidden access and performance of these services by later fathers because of their monthly flow that cannot be controlled.'[36] This continuing influence of the ancient purity laws of the First Testament—at least those concerning women—has never disappeared, even though it causes most Catholic people of today to cringe in shame.

When looking at Tradition, it is not only the quantity, but also the quality that must be considered. Some years earlier, Joseph Ratzinger himself had written:

> Not everything that exists in the Church must for that reason be also a legitimate tradition; in other words, not every tradition that arises in the Church is a true celebration and keeping present of the mystery of Christ. There is a distorting, as well as legitimate, tradition ... Consequently, tradition must not be considered only affirmatively, but also critically.[37]

---

[35] Kevin Madigan and Carolyn Osiek, *Ordained Women in the Early Church: A Documentary History*, Johns Hopkins Press, Baltimore, 2005, p. 137.

[36] Madigan and Osiek, op.cit, p. 138. I have quoted both these sources from Gary Macy's chapter in the book *Women Deacons*, Paulist Press, New York, 2011, pp. 31–32.

[37] Joseph Ratzinger, 'The Transmission of Divine Revelation', in *Commentary on the Documents of Vatican II*, vol.3, ed. Herbert Vorgrimler, Herder and Herder, New York, 1969, p. 185.

It is small wonder that Hans Kung responded to the reply of Cardinal Ratzinger by writing in an open letter to his friend, 'Joseph, how could you? You're far too good a theologian for this!'

The conclusion I have drawn from these events is that the declaration of papal infallibility in 1870 has now developed to the point that, in the Vatican, papal authority and infallibility trump all other issues. Popes of the past could not have been wrong in not ordaining women and that had to be the end of the matter or all papal authority would be called into question. So there could not even be any discussion, not among Catholic people throughout the world, and not within the Vatican itself. The only question remaining was how to suppress the talk by Catholic people on this subject. If this meant subjecting the desires, dignity and rights of women to the needs of papal authority, then so be it.

Since I believe that the exclusion of women from all positions of influence in the Church has been a significant causal factor in sexual abuse, this decision also means that the protection of papal authority and infallibility has been more important than eliminating sexual abuse.

It has also meant that, under the present system of governance within the Church, infallibility and collegiality are as incompatible as oil and water. The understanding of infallibility applied by Pope John Paul II in this case demanded monarchy. On any controversial issue a Pope could never guarantee that he would obtain that very high degree of consensus from the bishops that infallibility would demand. As long as this kind of infallibility reigns, there will be no room for collegiality.

And if the Pope is not listening to the bishops, then even less will he be listening to the whole Church. This in turn means that there will be no seeking of the opinion of women on any subject of importance, let alone on a subject such as sexual abuse where they might well have some strong things to say about how the Popes themselves and all the men around them have acted.

The male Church is another part of the unhealthy culture out of which abuse can arise and the response to abuse can be poor.

CHAPTER FIVE

A CULTURE OF CELIBACY

The predominant culture has not just been male, but celibate male, for all power has been in the hands of celibate males. In the atmosphere created by this fact, celibacy was the ideal, and the only concession made was that, in the words of Paul, 'it is better to marry than to burn' (1 Cor. 7:9), so that marriage was seen to involve an element of failure to strive for perfection.

Here I repeat what I said in my earlier book[38] concerning this subject:

> We must look well beyond celibacy if we are to find and eradicate the causes of abuse. Nevertheless, celibacy is all pervasive in the life of a priest and needs to be looked at in a special way.
>
> Among the many and complex causes of abuse, there are three categories in which celibacy appears to have made a direct contribution.
>
> While the abuse of children has been the object of almost all attention, there has also been abuse of adults, especially women, and this, too, has caused great harm to the victims. It has not received attention because the police have normally

---

[38] *Confronting Power and Sex in the Catholic Church: Reclaiming the Spirit of Jesus*, John Garratt Publishing, Melbourne, 2007, pp. 16–19.

responded that it appeared to be a consenting relationship and so no crime had been committed. In almost all cases, however, there had been the sexualising of a pastoral relationship, and in most cases an abuse of spiritual power, to obtain sexual favours. It is hard not to see celibacy as contributing to these cases of abuse of adult women.

There have been cases where persons have been taken into a seminary at too young an age and, because of the environment, their psychosexual development has not progressed beyond the age of about fifteen years, so that it is minors towards whom they are attracted. This is the explanation of only some cases of abuse, but they do exist.

In the third category, it is known that in an environment such as a prison, some heterosexual persons can become involved in homosexual sex, not by preference, but because it is all that is available. In a similar way, many priests have abused minors, not by preference, but because minors were available, either physically or psychologically. Physically, they have been available in places such as orphanages or schools where the offender worked. Psychologically, it is known that a number of offenders against minors claim that celibacy applies only to relations with adult women, so they claim in all seriousness that they have not broken their vow of celibacy. For some priests, this may be the sense in which adult women are psychologically 'not available', but minors are. Once again, this applies only to some cases and it would be foolish to think that with these three categories we had now explained all abuse.

In most cases it is not celibacy itself that is the problem, but obligatory celibacy. There have been saints who were so madly in love with both God and people that the idea of marriage did not even occur to them, for there was so much to do in loving people and caring for them that there would have been no time for marriage. A celibacy freely chosen out of a burning love for people is unlikely to lead to abuse, for it is not unhealthy.

The problem occurs when young persons are attracted to priesthood but find that it comes wrapped in a package that contains many elements. Because priesthood can exert such a powerful call, some of the other elements of the package, e.g. celibacy, do not receive the attention they should. The system of removing the candidates from the world and from 'temptation' does not assist them in this. Sometime after ordination, they can then find that priesthood still looks attractive, but celibacy does not. Sadly, many priests fall into this category. If the Pope were to ask for a disclosure 'before God alone' on this point from all priests, in secret and without betraying their identity, there might be both surprise and alarm at just how large is the number of those who are genuinely dedicated to the priesthood but are living it in an unwanted, unassimilated and, therefore, unhealthy celibate state. Many of those who have left the priesthood in the last forty years have been in this category, but so have many of those who remain.

All of this points to the major problem with obligatory celibacy, namely, that it is the attempt to make a free gift of God obligatory, and one must seriously question whether this is possible.

The law of celibacy assumes that everyone who is called by God to priesthood is also called by God to celibacy and given the divine assistance necessary to lead a celibate life. But is this a proven fact or a mere assertion? Is it a case of human beings making a human law and then demanding that God follow that law by giving special divine assistance to those bound by the law? If Church authorities really wish to insist on obligatory celibacy as a requirement for priesthood, should they do far more than simply assume a call to celibacy in those interested in the priesthood? Could they, for example, continue to take students into the seminary before they were adults and had an adult understanding of what celibacy means? May they continue to assert that those thousands of priests who have left the priesthood in recent decades in order to marry were all called by God to celibacy and given every divine help they needed, but deliberately refused this assistance?

Celibacy can also contribute to abuse in an indirect manner by contributing to the unhealthy psychological state (e.g. depression), the unhealthy ideas (e.g. misogyny or homophobia) and the unhealthy environment (e.g. an unwanted and unassimilated celibacy) out of which abuse arises. Though it is far from being the sole cause of abuse, it cannot be said that it makes no contribution. If the Church is serious about overcoming abuse, then the contribution of celibacy must be most carefully considered.

There is one other way in which celibacy has contributed to abuse. A significant reason why the response of many church authorities has been poor is that many bishops and religious superiors, not being parents themselves, have not appreciated just how fiercely, and even ferociously, parents will act to defend their children from harm. If they had been parents, there would surely have been a more decisive response.

At least in the Western world, celibacy has come to be seen as the acid test of whether the Church is truly serious about overcoming abuse. Much that is said can be simplistic and involve misconceptions, but this does not change the *fact that, unless and until the Church puts obligatory celibacy on the table for serious discussion, people will simply not believe it is serious about abuse. To start with the statement that the requirement of obligatory celibacy cannot and will not be changed or even examined, as both Pope John Paul II and Pope Benedict XVI have done, is to lose credibility before the discussion even begins. Some may speak all they wish of the benefits of this celibacy for the Church, but others will not stop asking, 'How many abused children is celibacy worth?'*

To this some further considerations can be added. The preparation for a life of celibacy in the seminaries was (and in most cases remains) negative ('Don't do this, avoid that'), and there was little assistance in building healthy friendships, especially with persons of the opposite sex. The only answer given to the problems this creates was that God would provide all the love and friendship one might need. And yet it is not enough for authorities to say that priests freely took on the obligation of celibacy, that divine love is abundant and that all that is needed is that they pray harder. This undervaluing of the importance of human love and friendship contains serious dangers.

Given sufficient motivation, some young persons might be prepared to embrace a life without genital sex, but no young persons in their right mind should ever embrace a life without love. Sadly, many priests are living their lives without a minimal sense of loving and being loved. This can lead, not only to one or other form of abuse, but also to the sadly common problems among priests of alcoholism, misogyny and ambition.

The better priests are as human beings, the better they will be as priests. Given the choice between better human beings who are married and less developed human beings who are celibate, I would choose the better human beings immediately. So one of the questions the Church must face is whether obligatory celibacy is harming the development of good human beings. The question is a most serious one and cannot be simply brushed aside.

Celibacy is a charism that, when freely embraced and accepted by the individual, can produce great gifts for the Church. The example of many saints shows this truth in a wonderful manner. The Church is on much more precarious ground, however, when this charism is institutionalized in law and required of a whole group of people who, even when sincerely striving to be good, are ordinary weak human beings, only some of whom have been or will be saintly. Sanctity is certainly a goal for every priest, but there is great danger in demanding something close to sanctity through law. The role of law always concerns the common good, and it is never the role of law to coerce the individual to be good. The covert sexual relationships that have always existed have been a source of great scandal.

It is sad that so many thousands of priests have resigned from ministry in order to marry, and their number includes many good and hard-working priests who could have given excellent service to the Church. It has become increasingly difficult to maintain that the charism has been there in every case and that the fault lies entirely with the individual.

When the other factors mentioned in this book are put together with an unwanted celibacy, the warning signs are too clear to be ignored.

CHAPTER SIX

THE MYSTIQUE OF THE PRIESTHOOD

The Letter to the Hebrews contains the sentence: 'Every high priest chosen from among human beings is put in charge of things pertaining to God on their behalf...'[39]

In the original Greek text, the word translated as 'chosen' is *lambanomenos*, which simply means 'taken'. The obvious meaning is that one human being exactly like all the others is chosen for the task of priesthood, just as others are chosen as teachers or nurses or community leaders. The Latin translation, however, that was used from the time of St. Jerome until just a few years ago, translated *lambanomenos* as *assumptus*, 'taken up', and from this developed a mystique of the priesthood as 'taken up' above other human beings.

This interpretation of the 'Letter to the Hebrews' is proven false by the very next words in that letter: 'He is able to deal gently with the ignorant and wayward, since he himself is subject to weakness, and because of this he must offer sacrifice for his own sins as well as for those of the people.'[40]

---

[39] Heb. 5:1.
[40] Heb. 5:2–3.

Despite this, the idea has persisted.

It has been reinforced by the statements in some quarters that through ordination the priest is 'ontologically different' from lay Christians, with the word 'ontologically' meaning 'in their very being'. No explanation is given as to what this means, and I confess that I have always found it meaningless. It appears to be another of those pure assertions that are made to bolster teachings that have little rational support, and one may once again apply the principle of logic that 'what is freely asserted may be freely denied'.

Furthermore:

> Since the time of Constantine the priesthood became a distinct professional unit, ultimately synonymous with 'officialdom' … In the Middle Ages this was to develop into a definition of ministerial priesthood in terms of the conferring of power. Yet, as Yves Congar explains, the defect of this approach is that it translates into a linear scheme: Christ makes the hierarchy and the hierarchy makes the Church as a community of faithful. Such a scheme, even if it contains part of the truth … places the ministerial priesthood before and outside the community[41]

In these facts there is a whole trend that is quite unhealthy. Countless Catholic people have experienced in priests an attitude of being taken up above others and being superior to them. It is exactly the kind of unhealthy idea that can contribute to abuse, and sexuality is only one of the areas in which priests can think that they are

---

[41] David Ranson ocsa, 'Priesthood, Ordained and Lay', *Australasian Catholic Record*, vol. 87.2 (April 2010), p. 152.

special, unlike other human beings and not subject to the restrictions that bind others.

The privileges of this mystique will always be attractive to many inadequate personalities. The mystique also gives priests privileged access to minors and a powerful spiritual authority over them, making it so much easier to abuse.

All sexual abuse is first and foremost an abuse of power. It is an abuse of power in a sexual form. Unhealthy ideas concerning power and its exercise are always relevant to the question of abuse.

If the governing image of how to act as a priest is tied to the ideas of lordship and control, an unhealthy domination and subservience will be present. If the idea of being called 'Father' is not taken from the Gospels, where it is invariably used as a term of intimacy and affection, and instead comes from the Roman concept of the *paterfamilias*, unhealthy and dangerous attitudes have been established.

The worst case is that of the 'messiah complex', where a person believes that God is calling him or her to be, as it were, a messiah: a chosen one who is called to some special mission and is, therefore, above the rules that apply to ordinary mortals. In such cases, if sexual abuse does not occur, some other form of abusive behaviour will. Every single priest needs to admit that the messiah complex is a real temptation that must be carefully and rigorously thrust aside.

Spiritual power is arguably the most dangerous power of all. In the wrong hands it gives the power to make judgements even about the eternal fate of another person. It needs a sign on it at all times saying, 'Handle with extreme care'. The greater the power a person exercises, the more need there is for checks and balances before it is used and accountability after it is used.

One of the saddest sights in the Church today is that of some young, newly-ordained priests insisting that there is an 'ontological difference' between them and laypersons and enthusiastically embracing the mystique of a superior priesthood. Whenever I see young priests doing this I feel a sense of despair, and wonder whether we have learned anything at all from the revelations of abuse.

PERFECTIONISM

Part of the mystique can be an inability to accept failure and vulnerability. Priests can feel that, because they have been 'taken up', they must be perfect. When they realise that they cannot achieve this, they can feel that they must at least appear to be perfect. Perfectionism is always dangerous, and it is particularly dangerous in a field as vast as the spiritual and the moral, where perfection is simply not possible for a human being. Feeling that one must appear to be perfect even when one knows that one is not, and being unable to admit to failure and weakness is an unhealthy attitude; inherent in it is the covering up of faults that do occur and a split between the private individual and the public persona. There must be room for a painful struggle towards maturity, with many mistakes along the way.

I will always remember feeling apprehensive when I had to confront a priest over his consumption of alcohol and being greatly relieved when he freely admitted the problem. But then, just when I thought I had succeeded in my mission, the real problem arose. The priest could freely admit to me that his drinking was out of control and welcome my assistance, but he could not bear the thought of the people of the parish finding out. He had always tried hard to be perfect, and he could not live with the idea that the people would become aware of his failure and weakness. We talked this over at length, but I eventually felt that I had no choice other than to agree to a solution that would see him get help without the parishioners becoming aware of any problem.

I contrast this with another priest whose alcoholism was so public that it could never have been hidden from the parishioners. Then one day the devoted housekeeper who had looked after him for many difficult years fell seriously ill. He immediately stopped drinking, joined Alcoholics Anonymous and looked after her attentively for two years until she died. He remained sober and became a wonderful apostle to those who had a problem with alcohol. When he died, he had one of the biggest funerals I can remember, as people responded to this 'wounded healer' whose story moved them.

The first priest could not climb down off his pedestal of perfection, while the second had long since abandoned all ideas of pedestals and had a far better understanding of who and what he was. It was this second priest, with all his obvious weakness, who, after he had stopped drinking, could be more authentic and could better present the message of Jesus Christ.

Sadly, priests can be made to feel that superiors, people in their parish, the media and the community at large will also demand that they be perfect and will strongly criticise any lack of perfection. They can be made to feel that what would be described as an understandable failure in another person would be called 'sickening hypocrisy' in them. These expectations can cause them to show externally a level of perfection that they know they do not possess. In both priests on the one hand, and in the community on the other, there needs to be change in the expectations that are present. Priests are ordinary human beings and, if either they or the community forget this, one kind of problem or another will be caused.

It was Voltaire who said that 'the perfect is the enemy of the good', and Alcoholics Anonymous has adopted this as a central truth in its response to the addictive process. When the Church, mainly through the law of obligatory celibacy, demanded that priests be perfect, it in fact set them up to act in heinous ways.

A major reason why the revulsion against the Catholic Church over abuse has been so great is precisely that for centuries the Church presented itself as the great and infallible moral guide that could tell everyone else what to do and threaten eternal punishment for anyone who did not bow down and obey. And now this Church—which so vaunted its own perfection—has been shown to have a rottenness at its core. When the school bully is exposed, the whole school rejoices!

If we are ever to come out of this crisis of abuse, there must be a far greater humility. We need to adopt the Second Vatican Council's idea of 'the pilgrim people of God': a community of ordinary, struggling people seeking to find their way towards God and making many mistakes along the way. This is the kind of community that God created in the People of Israel in the First Testament, and we would do well to imitate this model. The Church can help the world only if it works from within it, not if it tries to be above it; as one writer has put it, God is concerned with the world, not really with the Church as different from the world.[42]

It is never easy to change an ethos or mystique, but this one must change, for it denies the essential humanity of the priest and so establishes a series of false relationships at the heart of the community. Priests are ordinary human beings. This ought to be obvious to everyone; but authorities, priests and Catholic people all need to consider more closely this truism. I find that wherever there are priests trying to climb down from their pedestal, there are always, not only Church authorities, but also many Catholic people insisting that they climb right back up again. The insistence

---

[42] Johannes Metz, *Theology of the World*, Herder and Herder, New York, 1969, p.50, note 51.

that priests be perfect, or at least appear to be perfect, is very real. An extraordinary number of people believe the naïve idea that 'priests are celibate, so they don't really have sexual desires and feelings the way the rest of us do.'

Of all the causes of abuse, this mystique of the priesthood would have to be put high on the list, and there will be much work involved in overcoming it.

CHAPTER SEVEN

LACK OF PROFESSIONALISM

Over several decades there has been a strong move towards greater professionalism in most fields of human activity, but priests have limped a long way behind. In the light of all that has happened, there is a crying need that priests should rapidly catch up with the wider society in this field of being truly professional in all they do.

Among the elements that need serious and immediate consideration are the following.

SELECTION OF CANDIDATES

There is a need for better selection processes of candidates. There needs to be a wider selection panel, and a competent and reasonably full history of the candidate needs to be gathered. A psychological assessment should be mandatory, with appropriate safeguards to ensure that any written assessment does not fall into the wrong hands and is not used to harm the candidate in any way.

The practice of taking children into the seminary should be abandoned throughout the world. No one under the age of twenty-one should be taken into anything called a seminary or into any situation that includes the expectation of lifelong commitment.

TRAINING FOR HUMAN DEVELOPMENT

The training during seminary years should place as much emphasis on human development as on religious and priestly development, for you simply cannot have a good priest who is not first a good human being. As a bishop I received many complaints about priests, some justified, some not. I could not help noticing that most complaints concerned what I might call human qualities, e.g. rudeness, rather than specifically priestly qualities. All of the best priests I have known have been good human beings. And the sexual abuse of minors is something that would be totally foreign and repugnant to any half-way decent human being. If everything was done to ensure that every priest was as good a human being as possible, there would be much less abuse.

Seminaries have tended to concentrate on intellectual and spiritual formation alone, with little direct concern for human formation. Often, they have positively hindered such formation by creating an artificial and narrow world, largely turned in on itself. I will never forget the statement of a classmate of mine who, after leaving school, had worked for a number of years before entering the seminary. 'I went into the seminary a man, I came out a boy.'

Part of being taken 'out of the world' for training was the exclusion of women from any role in the seminary. Even the nuns who worked there and could have given great assistance to the students were not allowed to meet with them. There was a fear that if they met women, they would fall in love and want to leave. But an artificial world, in which women were excluded, became a poor place in which to grow to maturity.

> As long as seminaries and formation houses remain essentially unchanged, the church will have theologically literate priests and religious struggling with emotional and sexual illiteracy. Such people are candidates for sexual dysfunction [43]

In some places there have been some changes in seminaries, but by and large I find far too much of the old still in place. There is a serious need to look again at the entire system of training people for priesthood. The idea of taking candidates 'out of the world' and training them in intellectual and spiritual disciplines in a hothouse environment must be abandoned.

PSYCHOLOGICAL ASSESSMENT

Most priests currently working did not have a psychological assessment when they first entered the seminary. Whatever their present age, they can still benefit from a proper psychological assessment.

I had such an assessment some years ago. It confronted me with some unpleasant truths about myself, but I found the whole experience to be a liberating one. I finally understood certain things about myself: why I acted in certain ways, why I found some things difficult, why I had certain preferences; and this knowledge was liberating. It

---

[43] Davin Ranson, loc. cit.

was one of the best things I have ever done for myself, and I know that it helped me to be a better person and a better priest for others. If there were difficulties, I am glad I somehow found the courage to confront them.

In my case the assessment led me on to two years of counselling with a psychotherapist, so that I could better assimilate and deal with the matters that the assessment had revealed. I believe that this was also time well spent. Spending this amount of time and money on oneself is not selfish if it helps one to be a better human being, a better Christian and a better priest; for then, everyone benefits.

TRAINING FOR LEADERSHIP

The Second Vatican Council favoured a different form of the exercise of authority and for many people this became crystallised in the word 'leadership': the priest was to be a leader rather than a ruler.

Leadership is an art and there is much to learn in order to practice this art well. In the leadership course I did years ago we covered the following subjects:

- The Art of Christian Leadership
- Setting Goals
- The Task, the Team and the Individual
- Leadership Styles
- Qualities of a Leader
- Personality Types
- Methods of Decision Making
- Problem Solving

- The Group Climate
- Group Dynamics
- Personal Relationships
- Helpful and Destructive Behaviour
- Motivation
- Resolving Conflict
- The Challenge of Change
- Coping with Stress
- Time Management

The program was most helpful but was, of course, only a beginning, and one needs to continue learning throughout life. I do not understand why any priest would not want to do such a course. Training toward leadership surely needs to be an obligatory part of being a professional priest.

PROFESSIONAL APPRAISAL

In the past the only form of appraisal of priests came from the bishop and it tended to be negative. Most older priests have vivid memories of bishops who were quick to tell them about anything they had done wrong, but slow to offer a word of encouragement or support. As a consequence, many priests still have a negative view of any suggestion of appraisal.

So at the outset it needs to be said that a process aimed solely at finding faults and producing a critical and negative judgement is the very opposite of what is intended. On the contrary, a good appraisal will offer praise and support for all the good things in the priest's life and work and, where it strikes negatives, it will never present the negative without at the same time offering positive assistance in dealing with and overcoming that negative. The entire aim is to help the priest to become a better priest, not simply a more guilt-ridden one. A good appraisal will never use guilt as a motive for change.

For the same reason, an appraisal should never be used to deal with a particular problem. If, for example, a bishop becomes aware that a particular priest has a problem with alcohol, this problem should be confronted directly, not through an appraisal.

The appraisal can take many forms, but I suggest that the essential elements are these:

- The person to be assessed first writes out a personal understanding of a job description
- The person writes out an honest self-assessment of performance against this job description
- A panel with a good knowledge of the process of assessments is set up and a varied list of persons who know the priest is drawn up
- The panel sees to the questioning of these persons, asking them to comment on all aspects of the work of the priest, including any signs of harmful or dangerous activity
- The priest is interviewed
- The bishop or religious superior could be interviewed, and writings of the priest could also be asked for

- The panel then writes its appraisal and presents this to the priest in an interview.

The panel's sole aim in this is to assist the priest to be a better priest. Thus, as well as looking at issues of work, they would also look to see whether the priest takes adequate care of self, e.g. a regular day off each week, a holiday each year, and friends outside the parish—friends who can be just friends and towards whom there are no professional obligations.

The panel would then look at the job description given by the priest and assess whether it appears adequate or whether there are gaps in it. It would give much attention to the self-appraisal, for this would be at the heart of the entire appraisal. One way in which this is frequently expressed is to say that the purpose of the appraisal is to determine whether the priest's self-assessment is congruent with the assessment by the other persons who have given testimony.

In most professions, appraisals normally take place every four or five years, but parish priests are appointed for six years, so this appears to be a convenient measure. I suggest that the appraisal take place in the fifth year of a six year appointment, so that the priest would then have a year to work on anything in the appraisal that needs attention before applying for either a renewal of the appointment or a new appointment.

If a bishop wishes the priests of the diocese to have a regular appraisal, it would be absolutely essential that the bishop be the very first person in the diocese to have this appraisal, and that the priests be aware that this has been done.

In my own diocese, I was allowed to present these ideas concerning appraisals to the priests and offer the services of people who would be suitable panel members, but the bishop would not make it obligatory for the priests. The result was that a reasonably small number had an appraisal; and, generally speaking, those who least needed an appraisal had one, while those who would have benefited most did not. I believe that if the Church is to be seen to be truly serious about confronting abuse the appraisal should be as obligatory for priests as it is for most other professionals. For most other people the experience is that, after some initial difficulties, appraisals simply become part of the furniture.

I have had such an appraisal and, once again, while it had its difficulties, it was one of the most positive and helpful things I have ever done for myself. It gave me far more confidence in myself and my work than any words from a superior could have done.

PROVISIONS FOR CHILD PROTECTION

In each diocese there must be structures aimed precisely at the protection of children against all forms of abuse in a Church environment. The forms can vary, but will usually include the appointment of individuals to whom people can go in order to speak, not just about offences committed, but also about worrying signs of inappropriate behaviour that could be leading towards an offence.

There are what has been called 'red flags' of serious problems in a priest's life: e.g. a priest who seems to relate to children far better than to adults, a priest who cuts himself off from the company of fellow priests and becomes a loner, a priest with obvious signs of immaturity, a priest who is habitually abusive in manner in dealing with people, a priest who constantly needs to prove himself, a priest who seems to have abandoned any interest in a spiritual life, a priest who was himself abused as a child and has not been through a careful and professional process of resolving the abuse. The presence of one or even several red flags is not proof of any offence, and the absence of all red flags is not proof that a priest will not offend. At the same time, the red flags are signs that must be taken seriously. If they are confronted and dealt with early, offences of various kinds can be prevented and the priest helped to be a better priest.

These provisions are not meant to create a climate of fear and suspicion; they also serve to protect the priest from false accusations. A truly professional priest will welcome them.

BOTH A SPIRITUAL DIRECTOR
AND A SUPERVISOR

In accordance with its values, the Church has always strongly urged priests to have a spiritual director to assist in the development of their spiritual life and their practice of prayer. Needless to say, I support this. At the same time, there is also a need for a supervisor (definitely not the same person as the spiritual director) to assist in all other aspects of their life.

Within a week of my first arriving at my first parish a couple came to see me for assistance in adopting a child from a Catholic agency. I talked with them and formed the very strong impression that their motive was that they were having serious difficulties in their relationship and thought that a child might help to save their marriage. Even as a very young priest I knew that this was not good, but I needed to have someone with whom I could discuss how I had handled this situation, and a steady supervisor would have been ideal.

A year later, still in my first appointment, I was called down to a house where a couple's only child had just died in a cot death. Once again, a supervisor who could have helped me to learn from such an experience would have been of great assistance.

Even now that I have been a priest for over fifty years, situations are still constantly arising where the presence of a supervisor would enable me to be a better priest and to continue learning.

The supervisor should be someone who can be truly professional; possibly another priest, but someone respected rather than one's best friend who will always make affirming noises. In the years when I was heavily involved in responding to sexual abuse, I found that I needed a psychologist to be my supervisor and assist me in all the issues that arose. I did this in agreement with the priest who had been acting as my regular supervisor and I still reported to him on what was happening.

The arrangement I came to with the supervisor was that I would see him (the priest) or her (the psychologist) once a month, but could also call on the telephone if I felt that I needed more urgent assistance. The presence of a supervisor in my early years as a priest would have been at least equally beneficial as it has been in my later years.

The presence of a supervisor is standard in most fields of professional activity today, and once again I believe that it needs to be obligatory. Expenses incurred in supervision are a legitimate charge on the office the priest holds rather than on the individual.

IN-SERVICE TRAINING

In many other fields today—including the commercial—in-service training days are obligatory and simply part of one's job. The costs are paid by the employer. If a person does not attend and has no adequate excuse, this would count against the person when it came to a question of promotion or increase in salary.

This professional mentality needs to enter the lives of priests. In any job—and this most certainly includes the priesthood—there is always new knowledge to be gained and new skills to be learned. I have heard homilies that betray a knowledge of the Bible that has not been updated in fifty years, even though there have been huge developments in biblical research and understanding. I have heard priests who do not seem to have heard of the Second Vatican Council.

People deserve better than this.

Once again I would see this as obligatory, with promotion or renewal of an appointment (e.g. as parish priest) dependent on regular attendance.

A CODE OF CONDUCT

All truly professional bodies today have a Code of Conduct setting out the expected conduct of members in many commonly occurring situations. This, too, is new for priests and is by no means universal.

The Code for Australia—Integrity in Ministry— covers, among other areas, topics such as Developing and Maintaining Competence, Commitment to Justice, and Integrity in Administration.

In the Foreword it says of itself:

> A code of conduct is not intended to restrict or stifle the conduct of those professionals to whom it applies. Rather, it is a set of behavioural standards to ensure that professionals themselves preserve their own dignity and respect the human dignity of all to whom they relate in the exercise of their profession… It sets out behaviour for clergy and religious to integrate into their day-to-day ministry and serves as a check-list against which they can review the quality of the ministerial activities in which they engage.

The document goes well beyond the issue of sexual abuse, but it does set out provisions that, in the present context, every priest who wanted to remove even the faintest suspicion of abuse would carefully follow.

Any code of conduct must contain a section setting out the redress a person could have against a priest when the violation of the code has been egregious, and these provisions must extend to the bishop of the diocese as well as the priests.

It would be quite counterproductive if the bishops wrote a code of conduct and then imposed it on priests. The priests must be involved in the writing of the code and take ownership of it.

CLERICAL DRESS

The official dress for priests is still the formal black suit and clerical collar. In the modern world this makes priests seem different from all other human beings and out of touch with the world in which normal people live. Many priests have reacted against this and wear no uniform and it must be admitted that, in this process, many of them appear as drab, untidy and even scruffy.

In 1994, shortly after I was given the task of responding to accusations of abuse, I met with a group of about ten victims. In the midst of the discussion it happened that one of them spoke of the priest-abuser as a man who would never normally wear a black suit, but did so whenever he went out to abuse. To everyone's surprise, every single other member of the group then confirmed that exactly the same thing had happened to them. It was agreed that the abusers put on the black suit because it gave them maximum authority.

I have not worn a black suit since that day.

I know that changing from black to some other colour and changing from a clerical collar to a tie would never, by itself alone, overcome the image of abuse, but images are powerful and retaining the black suit is not helping.

The time has surely come to look again at the public image priests present through their manner of dress. A scruffy priest at a formal gathering is not a good image, but neither is a priest in a formal black suit and clerical collar at a parish picnic. I suggest the general principle that priests should dress with the same degree of formality or informality as good laypersons would in the same circumstances.

To allow for the diversity that this principle would bring into the manner in which priests dressed, I suggest that the clerical collar be replaced by a distinctive tie that would identify its wearers as priests without marking them as being a race apart.

RADICAL UNSUITABILITY

A further consideration needs to be added. It is not healthy that any group of people should believe that they have a job for life no matter what they do. The Code of Canon Law makes provision for the removal of a parish priest when his ministry 'has for some reason become harmful or at least ineffective, even though this occurs without any serious fault on his part.'[44] In the same way, there needs to be provision for the removal from priesthood altogether of the person who, even without fault, has shown a radical unsuitability for that life. There can be serious harm in keeping such a person within the priesthood. Yes, there would need to be stringent safeguards to prevent injustice, but the good of the people must come first.

The massive cloud of sexual abuse overshadows the Church and unambiguous steps need to be taken to show that the Church is serious about removing this cloud. A true professionalism in everything its ministers do is surely one of the first and most basic steps in this process.

---

[44] Canon 1740.

CHAPTER EIGHT

UNHEALTHY LIVING ENVIRONMENT

Some of the worst cases of abuse have occurred in orphanages and I suggest that there were two basic reasons why this happened.

Firstly, it is a universal rule that, the more powerless children are, the more abuse there will be—sexual, physical and psychological—and children in orphanages were particularly powerless. They had no family or anyone else to protect them, they had no redress against abuse and not even anyone to appeal to. They were at the total mercy of the staff, and all abuse could be concealed from anyone outside the orphanage. So the first conclusion is that Church personnel should not be involved with minors unless strong safeguards can be built in to ensure that the children are truly empowered and will not be exploited in the way they were in the past.

Secondly, a misguided sense of mission led a number of religious orders to undertake work in orphanages when they simply did not have the resources to carry out that work. On occasions it happened that those appointed to orphanages were the ones who did not have the ability to be teachers in schools or workers in more prestigious jobs, so they were the least qualified. They received no training, but were simply thrown into the job under 'holy obedience'.

Two different situations could arise. A single religious could be given the care of thirty young, and frequently disturbed, children; and would have this duty of care twenty-four hours a day seven days a week. There was no relief from the situation and no one outside the orphanage who could give support. This could cause such a level of stress for the carer that control of the noise and confusion created by the children became the overriding concern. This became a matter of sheer survival and there was no room for other considerations. A result was often particularly harsh discipline, and the way toward abuse had been opened.

The second situation that could arise was that the orphans had no one to love and, if allowed, could express deep affection towards their caregivers. For a celibate person, a young orphan's innocent show of affection could evoke a sexual response from the adult.

I am not seeking to excuse individuals from blame, for even in these situations there were always choices, but it is clear that in these circumstances a quite dysfunctional living environment contributed to abuse.

There are many stories in Church history of great saints who took on a particular mission, even when they had no money or personnel. They simply trusted in providence and their love conquered all obstacles. Such stories can be admirable, but in our own day we must reassess them in the light of all that has happened.

In speaking of celibacy, I warned of the dangers of

institutionalising a charism and demanding a saintly life of people who strive to be good but are not saints. In the same way, 'holy obedience' was not nearly enough for people who wanted to be good, but simply could not cope with the situation they were thrust into in orphanages. We cannot take the example of the greatest saints and impose it on ordinary people.

The normal living environment of the normal person is within a family. We are all aware of just how dysfunctional families can be: that is, just how poor the living environment can be for the children who grow up in that family. I worked full time in the field of broken marriages for seventeen years before I became a bishop and heard endless stories of just how bad families can be, so I do not look at marriage through rose-coloured glasses.

And yet, despite all of this, I believe that the family remains the best environment for most people to live in. When we move outside that environment, we must think very carefully about the forms of living we adopt.

With diminishing numbers, more and more priests are today living alone, and they are on call twenty-four hours a day, seven days a week. Each individual will respond to this situation differently, and some will cope far better than others. In itself, however, it is not a healthy environment, for it can lead to great loneliness and isolation, in which the emotional needs of the priest are not being met. In my work as a bishop I have been privileged to hear many personal stories of priests, and I have been greatly moved by stories of priests crying in their rooms because of the sheer loneliness of their lives. These priests cannot be simply dismissed as weak, and it is no answer to say that it is their own fault because they do not pray harder; answers like these are both insensitive and counterproductive, for they are simply a denial of the problem.

On the other hand, communities of priests such as are found in religious orders do not automatically solve all problems, especially if there are no real bonds of affection or even common interests. The physical presence of others is no guarantee of emotional support or of needs being met. One difficult member can disrupt an entire community. Precisely because they are all priests, there can be a demand for very high levels of behaviour at all times and unreasonable anger when they are not fully met. It is notable that larger religious communities are today frequently breaking up into smaller communities in order to avoid these problems, but some people can be left out in these arrangements.

A family based on the free choice of a partner and with bonds of genuine affection remains the best living environment for most people, and this would be true for priests also. If the decision is made not to have this environment, then much thought needs to be put into the alternatives that are adopted.

I am not concerned here to suggest alternatives, and I confess that this is in great part because I remain quite unconvinced that there are any adequate alternatives for those many priests who are celibate solely because a law tells them they have to be. I have no problem with the free choice of a celibate life by individuals, but I cannot see an adequate alternative lifestyle for all priests.

For as long as the law of celibacy remains in force, a great deal more work needs to be put into the question of the lifestyle of celibate priests, so that it does meet their most important human needs and enables them to live a sustainable human life. I cannot help wondering whether the obvious failure of the Church over many years to do this work is itself an admission that there is no adequate lifestyle that can be suggested for any priest who is not a saint or who has not freely embraced celibacy as a personal choice. In all of this, is there not far too much of the treating of people as Church authorities believe they ought to be rather than as they are?

Along with unhealthy psychological factors and unhealthy ideas, an unhealthy living environment has been one of the three factors that have contributed to abuse. If we are serious about overcoming abuse, a great deal more attention needs to be given to this factor.

PART TWO

Factors Contributing to the Poor Response

CHAPTER NINE

RIGHT BELIEFS V RIGHT ACTIONS

Over many years, tens of thousands of women in the United States have dedicated themselves to God in the Church as religious sisters. The vast majority have lived lives of obscurity, not performing newsworthy deeds and remaining unknown outside their immediate environment. They were not perfect, and yet they were in many ways the unsung heroes of the Church; their dedicated (and cheap) labour taught vast numbers of children, nursed patients in hospitals and reached out to the poor and needy in many communities. Even when we acknowledge their many defects, they built up a vast mountain of 'right actions', and the Catholic people of that country are aware of this history and of their own debt to these sisters.

In recent months, however, all of this appears to have been swept aside by the Vatican because of perceived deviations in 'right beliefs'. Its actions have been heavy-handed and authoritarian, with little attempt at dialogue. Some years after their publication, the books of two sisters—Sr. Elizabeth Johnson and Sr. Margaret Farley—have been condemned as containing theological errors, though many people (including myself) have found the two books both scholarly and helpful. Many observers have concluded that for the Vatican the molehill of 'wrong beliefs' is far more important than the mountain of 'right actions'. The Catholic people of that country, on the other hand, would give far more importance to the mountain of right actions, maintaining that this is far closer to the essence of the Christian faith.

I am not suggesting that right beliefs be simply ignored, but we need a far better balance between beliefs and actions. In the case of the American religious sisters, this would at the very least mean a greater, more open and more generous appreciation of the immense good they have done, and a more sensitive dialogue concerning deviations in beliefs and the manner in which they are to be dealt with.

In 2010, a pregnant woman was brought into a Catholic hospital in Phoenix, Arizona, with serious complications. The doctors studied all aspects of the case and concluded that it was simply impossible for them to save the child, despite their best efforts and despite all the advances of modern medicine. On the other hand, if they did nothing and simply let nature take its course, the mother would also die, and she had other small children to look after. Sister Margaret Mary McBride was part of the ethics committee of the hospital and she concluded that, rather than see both mother and child die, it was better to save the mother by removing the doomed foetus. This was an honest decision in conscience in a very difficult situation. The bishop of the diocese promptly excommunicated her for approving of and enabling an abortion.

And yet no paedophile priest in the United States has ever been excommunicated, and no bishop has ever been excommunicated for covering up the crime and allowing offenders to abuse more minors. Once again: right beliefs have been seen as far more important than right actions.

Once again, Catholic people have seen this as an upside down scale of values. They believe that Sr. McBride was faced with an acute moral dilemma, a situation without a win-win solution, and that she acted in good conscience. On the other hand, they believe that the entire saga of sexual abuse has been a complete disaster, with thousands of decisions that could not possibly have been in good conscience and that have caused untold harm to victims.

Far too often right beliefs have been put before right actions. If a priest is loyal to all papal teachings, his moral 'mistakes' can easily be forgiven. But if he is not loyal to even one teaching, no amount of good actions will redeem him, and his entire life of devoted service can be swept aside. A paedophile priest can be forgiven, but not someone who is unsound on contraception or the ordination of women.

Other religions have not fallen into this trap. Jews, Muslims and Buddhists, for example, pay far less attention to right beliefs and far more to right actions. It has become a peculiarly Catholic phenomenon.

It is one more part of the unhealthy culture I am seeking to describe. As long as one is faithful to Church teachings, any wrong actions one performs can be easily forgiven. The accent on right beliefs has inevitably led to a downplaying of the importance of right actions. This in turn has led to a downplaying of the extreme seriousness of the sexual abuse of minors, for acts of abuse are 'only' wrong actions that are easily forgiven, and not nearly as important as wrong beliefs.

UNLIMITED FORGIVENESS

Part of the problem has been the belief of the Church in unlimited forgiveness by God of all human offences, for this belief has not made the absolutely necessary distinction between unlimited forgiveness of past offences and the prevention of foreseeable future offences. At a meeting in the Vatican in 2000 on sexual abuse, I vividly remember being told publicly by a Roman Cardinal, 'You are not a Christian, you do not believe in forgiveness!' In this belief, all wrong actions, no matter how heinous and no matter what harm they have caused to others, can be forgiven, swept aside and forgotten, and any limitation on this for the purpose of preventing future offences was a refusal of full forgiveness. This attitude was part of the poor response to abuse: in the name of forgiveness, essential steps to prevent further abuse were not taken. If an offender said he was truly repentant and would not offend again, forgiveness meant that the presumption was in his favour. As a result, offenders were moved from place to place and could offend again.

This attitude has been changing as realisation of the extreme harm caused through abuse has grown, but historically it has been a significant cause of the poor response, and I cannot be sure it no longer exists.

PROTECTING THE INSTITUTION

Protecting the good name of any institution or society one belongs to is a universal human phenomenon. One sees it in families, clans, tribes, nations, governments, political parties, commercial enterprises, football clubs and, indeed, any group where people come together and invest their energy and good name. A Church, however, is particularly vulnerable to this danger, for it feels more strongly that it is essential that it appear perfect. Like the priest I mentioned earlier who desperately wanted help to overcome his addiction to alcohol but could not bear the idea of the members of the parish thinking of him as failing, so the Catholic Church could not bear to be seen as failing, and far too often this became the dominant attitude in its subsequent actions.

And yet, not merely did it fail, but it failed monstrously through thousands of cases of its elite priests committing the utterly despicable crime of the sexual abuse of helpless minors, and countless cases of even more elite bishops putting the good name of the Church before the victims of these crimes. The scandal has been so massive that it has led even the best of Catholics to feel that there is something rotten at the heart of the Church. To speak only of wrong actions by individuals is seen as a shuffling of deckchairs on the *Titanic*. If right beliefs continue to be seen as far more important than even this scale of wrong actions, the Church would have little future. To overcome this scandal, it must look at itself again from the foundations up, and that must include looking at laws and beliefs such as those I have already mentioned.

BEING THEOLOGICALLY 'SAFE'

Over the last thirty years, the placing of beliefs before actions has also meant that the choice of bishops has depended largely on whether they were seen as theologically 'safe'. And yet I suggest that this is less important than whether they are genuine Christians and warm human beings, whether they have a thirst for justice and are filled with compassion. One of my major criticisms of theologically 'safe' appointments is that such bishops tend to relate to people from a stance of authority rather than as real and warm human beings; a concern for right beliefs over right actions seems to prevent them from being real human beings. If you put one of these 'safe' bishops in front of a classroom of senior high school students to answer their questions about religion, life and morality, the human being can quickly disappear in favour of the stern authority insisting on the party line.

The large number of these appointments also means that the concern for right beliefs over right actions will be even stronger than it was before. Over the very years that have seen the revelation of so many cases of abuse, more and more bishops have been appointed whose overriding concern is that the Church could never be wrong in its beliefs, so these beliefs can never be looked at again. This helps to explain my earlier statement that no Pope has even called for a profound study of any and all factors within the Church that might have contributed either to abuse or to the poor response.

One of the most important failures of the Church today is the failure in the crucial battle for the imagination of people. Too many people, including large numbers of good Catholics, find that when they look at the Church they feel no enthusiasm and their imaginations are not fired. Heavy bishops who put beliefs before actions inspire no one, and, tragically, even Jesus can be made to look boring. A failure to provide a comprehensive response to abuse then takes away the last shred of inspiration. In vast numbers, the youth of today find themselves looking elsewhere for their inspiration and enthusiasm.

Sadly, so do large numbers of older people like myself.

The story of Jesus is exciting, and if we fail to communicate that excitement, we are failing in our primary task. And a Church that prizes beliefs before actions will inevitably fail in that task.

A fundamental change that the Vatican has singularly failed to appreciate is that the Catholic people of today are far better educated than they were centuries ago. In earlier times people may have been more willing to follow authority, but today they look for reasoned arguments for any position proposed. When the Church relies on authority alone rather than arguments, and insists on right beliefs above all, the lines of communication break down.

This reflects the unhealthy idea that faith is essentially intellectual assent to propositions rather than a response of my whole being to God's love. We need to remember that Jesus said: 'By this shall all know that you are my disciples, that you love one another',[45] and not 'that you all recite the same Creed and obey the same Pope.'

---

[45] John 13:35.

CHAPTER TEN

PAPAL INFALLIBILITY AND PRESTIGE

In theory, infallibility covers only a very restricted number of teachings solemnly proclaimed by the Pope. In practice the mantle of infallibility extends to cover many other matters as well. In a phenomenon that has been called 'creeping infallibility', it extends to cover all teachings, laws and practices in which a significant amount of papal energy and prestige have been invested.

A classic example is the teaching on birth control. The encyclical *Humanae Vitae* lacked the technical requirements of infallibility. And yet so much papal energy and prestige have been invested in this teaching that for many people it is quite unthinkable that the Pope could be wrong, for such an admission would seriously undermine all papal prestige, and that can never be allowed to happen.

The same can be said for other matters I have raised in this book. It would be devastating to papal prestige to have to admit that, over a period as long as two thousand years, Popes had been wrong in not ordaining women. It would be intolerable to have to admit that on a subject as basic to human life as sexual morality the Popes had failed to understand. It could never be admitted that God might see homosexuality in a manner different from that of the Popes. It could not be admitted that the imposition of celibacy on every single priest over many centuries had not been wise. And there have been many other examples under Popes John Paul II and Benedict XVI.

In my earlier book I spoke of 'the prison of the past'. I suggested that, in declaring the Pope infallible, the Church had built a prison for itself, locked itself in and thrown away the key. I said that I could surrender many of my rights and still live a good life, but I could not survive for a day without my right to be wrong. I demand the right to say, 'I'm sorry, I failed to understand', 'I'm sorry, I was insensitive.' The Church absolutely needs this same right and cannot live without it.

And yet the entire response of the Church to the scandal of sexual abuse has taken place in this atmosphere that the Pope cannot have been wrong in any matter that involved papal energy and prestige. This has had a crippling effect on the entire response. Abuse has called papal prestige into question in a way that few other things have, and it is manifestly impossible to give an adequate response while maintaining that the Pope (and, therefore, the Church) cannot have been wrong in his response or in any of the factors that may underlie the scandal.

No Pope has ever even called for a profound study of any and all factors that may have contributed to the scandal of abuse, for every Pope knows that an honest study might lead to powerful calls to change laws, practices and even teachings in which much papal prestige has been invested.

It is a sad fact that, even at this stage of the abuse

crisis, there are still things within the Church that are considered more important than responding to abuse, and the very first among them is papal authority and prestige. When papal infallibility was solemnly declared as a dogma at the First Vatican Council in 1870, it was thought that it would answer certain problems of the time. But the tail has come to wag the dog, and everything in the Church must now be adapted and compromised in order to defend papal infallibility.

Because infallibility was controversial even at the time it was declared, and remains so today, the need to defend it at all times and in all places has been strongly felt by those in authority. Everything else has been subjected to it, as I demonstrated regarding the ordination of women. Whether the question be contraception, the ordination of women, sexual morality in general or homosexuality in particular, or any other matter into which the Pope has poured any measure of papal prestige, the discussion quickly ceases to be a discussion of that topic and becomes a discussion of papal authority.

The Pope has even been unable to ask the whole Church for help, for he can never guarantee what answer the Church might give and what teachings might be called into question.

Arguably, this has been the major force in preventing a Pope from making admissions that there have been serious failures in the handling of abuse, or even from allowing discussion of issues such as those I raise in this book. If we are looking for the causes of the poor response to abuse, this one must be put at the top of the list.

LOYALTY TO A SILENT POPE

Before ordination as a bishop, every candidate is required to take an oath of loyalty to the Pope: not God, not the Church, but the Pope. Every bishop is meant to be 'a Pope's man', and bishops take this oath seriously.

If, when accusations of abuse first arose, the Pope had made a public statement telling bishops to respond fearlessly and openly, always putting victims before the good name of the Church, I believe it would have had a powerful effect.

Accusations of abuse first came to public notice in the early 1980's, and for the following twenty years the Pope was Pope John Paul II. Sadly, it must be said that he responded poorly. For twenty crucial years loyalty equalled loyalty-to-a-largely-silent-Pope, so silence and concealment became the response of 'loyal' bishops.

I cannot guarantee that every bishop would have followed his lead if the Pope had spoken out; what I believe I can state with conviction is that the powerful loyalty to the Pope of all bishops would have worked in favour of victims, whereas his silence meant that this loyalty worked against them.

With authority goes responsibility. Pope John Paul many times claimed the authority; he must accept the responsibility. The most basic task of a Pope is surely to be the 'rock' that holds the Church together and, by his silence in the most serious moral crisis facing the Church in our times, the Pope failed in this basic task. I felt that the demand was being made that I give my 'submission of mind and will' to the silence as well as to the words of a Pope, and in the matter of abuse I could not do this.

The beatification of this silent Pope has been another blow to all victims.

A CULTURE OF SECRECY

Within Italy there is a powerful culture of *bella figura*. The phrase literally means 'a beautiful figure' and its opposite is *brutta figura*, an 'ugly figure', and the two phrases occur frequently in Italian conversations. The real meaning of *bella figura* is that of always presenting a good external appearance to the world, while *brutta figura* means a failure to do this, allowing less desirable features to be seen behind the façade. The idea is profoundly entrenched, for it was already powerful two thousand years ago in the Roman Empire. Those imbued with that culture would have serious difficulties in ignoring it and speaking openly about faults.

I was a student in Rome in 1960 when the Olympics were held in that city. As the time approached, many things were not nearly ready. So in the week before the athletes started arriving, an army of men was sent out with buckets of white paint to cover everything in sight. In this way, as long as the athletes did not jump too hard on anything, *bella figura* would be preserved.

For many centuries this idea of *bella figura* has been reflected in the secrecy that has been an important part of the culture of the Vatican. Wrong actions can easily be pardoned, and the unpardonable sin is that of making those wrong actions public. I speak here from personal experience, for a bishop guilty of the sexual abuse of an adult female was actually promoted while I was rebuked for criticising the Vatican's handling of the matter.

The Acts of the Apostles show that Peter, the first Pope, was not above criticism and had to answer to the Church for his actions.[46] Today, on the contrary, the Pope is held to be above criticism, is not answerable to the Church and must be protected and defended in every way possible. The latest symptom of this is the statement from the Vatican Press Office (28 June 2010): 'It must be reiterated that, in the Church, when accusations are made against a cardinal, competency falls exclusively to the Pope.' The words and deeds of cardinals reflect on the Popes who appointed them, so no one else may be allowed to criticise them.

This culture of obsessive secrecy has been a powerful factor in the mishandling of abuse.

It is a sad fact that, if the Church has been slow to respond properly to abuse, the slowest part of all has been its central bureaucracy. In being so defensive, blaming the media, regarding the fairness of the way the Church has been treated as the central issue, protesting that the

---

[46] Acts 11:1–18.

Church is better than other organisations that have got off lightly, defending the Pope at all costs and dissociating the Church from wrongdoers within it, various members of that bureaucracy have shown that they have missed what truly matters.

The response to abuse must be total. In seeking to abolish both abuse and the poor response, we must be free to follow the argument wherever it leads, and we cannot place obstacles in the way. We cannot say, 'We must not even discuss this point because such and such laws or teachings prohibit it' or 'We cannot even discuss that other point because it would affect papal authority and prestige.'

It is precisely this attitude—more than anything else—that has, I believe, got in the way of a full, honest, humble and compassionate response to both abuse and the poor response to abuse.

PART THREE

Enabling a Healthy Response

CHAPTER ELEVEN

THE COLLEGE OF BISHOPS

In some places, the Second Vatican Council says that the college of bishops (all the bishops of the world including the Pope) possesses supreme and full authority over the universal Church, and in others that the Pope alone possesses supreme and full authority.

It is difficult to maintain the idea of two bodies (the Pope alone and the college of bishops) holding the same supreme power within a community without creating a tension between the two bodies, and it is inevitable that one or the other will in practice dominate; that one will in fact be supreme and the other will not. In the time since the Council, it has been evident that—in fact and in practice—the Pope has possessed supreme power, while the college of bishops has not. I commented on this conflict in speaking about the ordination of women in an earlier chapter.

Despite this conflict, it is always possible for the Pope to consult the bishops. The Council spoke of three ways in which this could happen:

- a Council
- a summoning to collegiate action by the Pope

- a collegiate initiative by the bishops themselves that is approved or freely admitted by the Pope.

I shall consider the second and third option before the first.

A SUMMONING TO COLLEGIATE ACTION BY THE POPE

The only ongoing expression of collegiality that was set up after the Second Vatican Council was the Synod of Bishops. This is held every three years or so. Some two hundred bishops are elected by the bishops around the world to represent them. The Pope then appoints another fifty or so bishops and a number of observers, so that the total number of those meeting is about three hundred. They discuss a particular topic for three weeks and draw up and vote on resolutions.

I have attended three synods and I found that, while agreeing that the synod is much better than nothing, many of those who were present had serious reservations about it. All the bishops of the world do not get to vote on the resolutions, so many of those present did not see it as a real expression of full collegiality. The bishops do not publish their own resolutions, but hand them all over to the Pope, and a year or so later he publishes a document in the name of the synod. It is clearly stated that the synod has only an advisory authority: that is, it can give advice to the Pope, but it cannot publish decisions on its own or tell the Pope what to do. Many of those I spoke to felt that this process left little real power in the hands of the bishops.

My experience is that synods can be a good forum for the discussion of pastoral and practical matters, but are not really the place for the determining of matters of belief.

In its present form, I do not see the synod as the place for the discussion and resolution of the matters I have put forward in this book.

A COLLEGIATE INITIATIVE BY THE BISHOPS

In theory the bishops can ask for a collegiate action between themselves and the Pope in order to respond to some particular problem. In practice the bishops have not done so on the issue of abuse, and there is no indication that they have any intention of doing so.

Bishops take their oath of loyalty to the Pope seriously, and are very quickly reminded of it if they seem to stray. In light of this, I cannot see any likelihood of the bishops of the world telling the Pope that they are not satisfied with his handling of the abuse crisis. Bishops may complain about the cardinals and others who advise the Pope in the Vatican (the Roman Curia), but never about the Pope himself.

The Pope and the Curia have by now had some thirty years to take decisive steps to eradicate abuse but they have not done so, and it is impossible to have any confidence that they are about to do so now. Bishops could collectively have insisted on a far stronger response from the Pope, but their oath of loyalty so constricts them that not even together have they protested. Sadly, I do not see solutions coming from this source.

A COUNCIL

The last three Councils of the Catholic Church have been the Council of Trent (1545–1563), the First Vatican Council (1869–1870) and the Second Vatican Council (1962–1965). They have been rare events that sought to look at all aspects of the Church at a particular moment in history.

There is, however, no necessity for Councils to be of this kind; there is no reason why a Council cannot be called to deal with only one specific question that demands an answer; there is no reason why there could not be a Council to deal with the one question of abuse and the poor response to abuse.

The Second Vatican Council spoke of '...the holding of Councils in order to settle conjointly, in a decision rendered balanced and equitable by the advice of many, all questions of major importance.' (no.22)

The question of abuse is obviously 'of major importance', for it is crippling the entire mission of the Church and will continue to do so until it is confronted and eliminated. The matter would certainly benefit from 'the advice of many', so that the decisions arrived at would be 'balanced and equitable'. If we adopt these principles, a Council to eradicate sexual abuse becomes obligatory.

Since neither the Pope and the Roman Curia, nor either of the other forms of collegiate action offer serious hope of a solution, and since the matter continues to be 'of major importance', I suggest that we must turn towards the idea of a Council.

CHAPTER TWELVE

THE *SENSUS FIDEI* OF THE WHOLE CHURCH

The Second Vatican Council spoke of the *sensus fidei* (sense of faith) or *sensus fidelium* (sense of the faithful)—that instinctive sensitivity and power of discernment that the members of the Church collectively possess in matters of faith and morals.[47]

The People of God as a whole would never have allowed the Church to be where it is today over the issue of abuse, for their *sensus fidei* would have insisted on a far more rigorous and, dare I say it, Christian response. It is their children who have been abused and it is they who have had their faith weakened or destroyed. They would have been far fiercer in protecting children than the bishops have been. They have even, in one way or another, had to pay for the mess. The Pope and the bishops have lost credibility and it is only the People of God who can restore it to them. If the Church is to move forwards, these painful lessons must be learned, for this is an issue on which the sidelining of the People of God has been positively suicidal.

---

[47] *Lumen Gentium*, no.12.

The Latin term *sensus fidei*[48] is a good one because, while it includes rational thinking, it is in itself a sensing, an instinct, an intuition, a head-and-heart discernment of truth.

It is an ancient idea that had fallen into disuse until the Second Vatican Council revived it. The first draft documents followed a traditional pattern by speaking first of the Pope and then working down through the various levels of the Church until they reached the laity. The Council changed this, so that its final document speaks first of the mystery of the Church, then of the People of God, and only then of the hierarchy of the Church. In other words, the Church is first a work of God and a means of God's presence, then it is a community of people, and then, and only then, it is a community with a structure and a hierarchy within it in order to carry out its task. In its essence, the Church is a divine mystery and a pilgrim people, and structure and hierarchy cannot be given the same essential importance.

It was within this context that the Council made the statement that 'the whole body of the faithful ... cannot err in matters of belief.'[49] Because of the disagreements within the Council, however, conflicting ideas were placed side by side, so that the whole message given by the Council was that the body of the faithful cannot err in matters of belief, but in coming to these beliefs it must

---

[48] Both of the terms *sensus fidei* and *sensus fidelium* are in common use. *Lumen Gentium* speaks of the *sensus fidei*, so that is the term I shall use here.

[49] *Lumen Gentium*, no. 12.

follow the teaching authority of the Pope and bishops.[50]

Despite these ambiguities and conflicts, we must affirm that the Council clearly reintroduced the concept of the *sensus fidei* into Church thinking, and it cannot be made to go away.

We would also have to say that the solution to the conflicts present in the Council documents cannot lie in embracing only one side of the conflict. On the one hand, it cannot lie in seeing the *sensus fidei* of the People of God as above or independent from the Pope and bishops; on the other hand, it cannot lie in so subjecting the *sensus fidei* to the Pope and bishops that it is meaningless. It is a new synthesis that is required.

The essence of this synthesis must surely lie in the idea of dialogue. There must be dialogue between the Pope and the people, a dialogue that will enable the sensus fidei to be heard.

On the subject of sexual abuse, this dialogue would demand that the laity have a major voice in the Council I have proposed. The Pope and bishops have lost credibility because of the manner in which they have mishandled the entire issue of abuse. This loss has been so great that a Council consisting of only bishops would face a serious question of credibility. The problem has been compounded by the careful selection of more conservative priests to the role of bishop under the last two Popes, so that one must query the extent to which the bishops represent the whole

---

[50] See the whole text of both no.12 and no.25 of *Lumen Gentium* taken together.

Church. At this moment in the history of the Church—and on this issue—the bishops need the laity as they have never needed them before. In its simplest terms, statements by bishops alone, even in Council, would lack credibility; while statements of the whole Church would have much greater credibility. So the Council must in some manner include the whole Church. Indeed, the process of involving the entire Church would be at least as important as the written outcomes of the Council.

I suggest that the aim of the council would be to discover and articulate the faith and practice of the entire Church in response to the revelations of sexual abuse. I therefore suggest that the entire Church take part in the Council, but in such a manner that the members of the Church contribute in different ways according to the particular expertise and experience that they have, and with different people playing different roles.

There are precedents in Church history for people other than bishops attending a Council and having a vote. For example, at the Council of Florence (1435–42) three estates were present: bishops, abbots and religious, and 'lower clergy'. There is no reason why there cannot be significant numbers of non-bishops, especially laity, appointed as members of this new Council.

I am not concerned here to present a fixed plan for such a Council, but in the next chapter I shall attempt to show that a new type of Council is at least possible, and so to start a conversation concerning how it would work.

CHAPTER THIRTEEN

A NEW COUNCIL FOR A NEW CHURCH

So great has been the scandal of the sexual abuse of minors and so catastrophic have been its effects on every aspect of the work of the Church that I believe that there needs to be a Council of the whole Church to deal with the one subject: the eradication of this evil. Nothing less than this would be adequate when seen in the light of the gravity of the situation.

It must be a Council unlike any before it. There are four things in particular that must make it different.

1. SCOPE AND DURATION OF THE COUNCIL

The last three Councils (Trent, Vatican I and Vatican II) looked at all aspects of the Church at particular moments in history. It may well be argued that, in seeking to do this, the Second Vatican Council tried to cover too many subjects in too brief a period of time, with the consequence that it left many matters unresolved and was distinctly ambiguous on a number of others, leading to conflicting opinions concerning how it was to be interpreted.

This new Council must have the carefully limited and strictly determined focus of the eradication of sexual abuse. It would deal with only those factors within the Church that may have contributed either to abuse or to the poor response to abuse. The Council must then have the time to do its work thoroughly.

2. THE METHOD OF COMMUNICATION AND DISCUSSION

Each session of the Second Vatican Council brought together in Rome more than three thousand people, including the bishops, theological experts, secretaries and ancillary staff. The number of bishops has doubled over the last fifty years, so the number of people travelling to Rome for a Council today would be over six thousand. Bringing all these people to Rome and lodging them there for months on end would be both a logistical nightmare and prohibitively expensive. St. Peter's Basilica itself would be too small for the daily sessions.

The essence of a Council of the Catholic Church is that the unity of the Church be expressed through the calling of the Council by the Pope, that the subject matter of the Council be clearly determined, that there be a dialogue between the voting members of the Council and the relevant experts in each field, that through this dialogue—and their own sharing of information and opinions—the members have adequate opportunity to inform themselves on the issues, and that they then cast their votes.

It is not essential that they all come together in the one place at the one time in order to do this, for abundant discussion can take place both at more local levels and through the use of modern means of communication. In particular, every effort should be made to ensure that all members of the Council had available to them a personal computer and access to the internet. The majority of communication and access to materials would be through this means, and most discussions would be through this means; any other means of communication would have to be justified.

Special provisions would have to be made for those for whom access to the internet was not possible, but this has become a very small number, and it would seem wrong to say that we should not have a Council at all because of this small percentage.[51]

3. THE PARTICIPATION OF THE ENTIRE CHURCH

Since we can, through the means of communication available, avoid the financial and logistical problem of bringing them all together in Rome, I suggest that, for every eligible bishop there should be a non-bishop as well. This would mean a Council of around 10 000 members.

Among the non-bishops chosen a certain percentage (e.g. 10%) could be priests and religious, but the large majority would be laity.

The non-bishops could be chosen from among those who have done the equivalent of at least three years full time theological study at a recognised theological faculty. If

---

[51] Papua New Guinea is neither rich nor developed, and yet I know from personal experience that its bishops have access to the internet.

there are not enough suitable candidates in a particular area with this qualification, the requirement could be lowered to the equivalent of at least two years full time theological study, but not below this.

They should not be chosen from either the extreme conservative or the extreme progressive wing of the Church; that is, they should not be people who would start with the answers, but people who would humbly seek God's truth on each question, and would be prepared to change their minds whenever the evidence led them to do so.

All appointments should be strictly on merit, so that the Council might have the very best persons available to it. There has, however, been a long history in the Catholic Church of men being privileged over women in this as in every other field. Where two candidates are seen as equal, preference should, therefore, be given to a woman over a man, so that the number of women at the Council might come as near as possible to that of the men.

4. THE PRESUMPTION

At the very outset the Council would need to decide where the presumption and the burden of proof lie. The presumption can lie in favour of what has been believed or done in the past, and then it would require a consensus or at least a majority to change that belief or practice. Or it can lie in favour of the freedom of the children of God, and then it would require a consensus or at least a majority to reimpose an existing obligation or to impose a new one. It would certainly seem that the presumption should here, as in all fields, be in favour of freedom, but in order to avoid confusion this must be one of the first questions the Council decides.

These would be the overriding principles of the Council. A number of more detailed suggestions are included in this book as an Appendix.

CHAPTER FOURTEEN

THE VOICE OF THE PEOPLE OF GOD

I do not see either the Pope or the bishops as a whole being willing to call a Council on their own initiative in order to seek to eradicate abuse. Roman authorities are too concerned with preserving past teachings and practices, too concerned with papal power and prestige, too wedded to right-beliefs before right-actions, and too afraid of what an open Council on this subject would demand. Many bishops share these concerns, and all bishops are so constrained by their oath of loyalty that they are unwilling to speak strongly to the Pope in demanding a Council.

It is, therefore, to the *sensus fidei* of the entire People of God that I turn. Sexual abuse has made Catholic people feel sick to their soul each time a new story of abuse is told and deeply ashamed to be in any way associated with such unspeakable evil, so there is a profound energy for change among them. If Popes and bishops seem more concerned with right beliefs, the Catholic people are appalled by all the wrong actions and are demanding change. What is needed now is to gather all this energy and channel it.

Catholic people have not been used to telling bishops, let alone Popes, what to do, but on the issue of abuse that is definitely changing. They have become intensely critical of the bishops and are not satisfied with verbal apologies from the Pope or, indeed, with any response that consists of mere words.

What is needed is such a groundswell of public opinion by the Catholic people around the world that it eventually becomes a roar that even the Pope would hear. To achieve this, I would like to see millions of Catholic people from many countries signing a petition similar to the following.

PETITION FOR A COUNCIL

We, the undersigned members of the Catholic Church, have been sickened by the continuing stories of sexual abuse within our Church, and we are appalled by the accounts of an unchristian response to those who have suffered. When so many people either offend or respond poorly, we cannot limit ourselves to blaming individuals, but must also look at systemic causes. The situation is so grave that we call for an Ecumenical Council to respond to the one question of doing everything possible to uproot such abuse from the Church and produce a better response to victims. An essential part of this call is that the laity of the whole world should have a major voice in the Council (for it is our children who have been abused or put at risk), and that the following subjects be included:

- Seeking to remove all elements of a religion based on fear
- Immaturity in moral thinking
- The teaching of the Church on sexual morality
- The part played in abuse by celibacy, especially obligatory celibacy
- The need for a strong feminine influence in every aspect of the Church
- The idea that through ordination the priest is taken above other people (clericalism)

- True professionalism in the lives of priests and religious
- Unhealthy situations in which priests and religious can be required to live
- Right beliefs being seen as more important than right actions
- Secrecy and the hiding of faults within the Church, especially in the Vatican
- Ways in which the protection of papal authority has been put before the eradication of sexual abuse
- The provision of structures to make a reality of the 'sense of faith' (*sensus fidei*) of all Catholic people
- The need for each Conference of Bishops to have the authority to compel individual bishops to follow common decisions in this matter.

If change is to occur, it is the people who must now speak!

**SIGN THE PETITION
change.org/forchristssake**

APPENDIX

PRACTICAL SUGGESTIONS

I suggest three commissions at three levels to coordinate and carry forward the work of the Council.

The Central Commission

The federations of bishops' conferences could nominate members to a Central Commission of the Council (e.g. four from Western Europe, two from Eastern Europe, three from Africa, five from South America, two from North America, and three from Asia and Oceania together, equalling seventeen). To this there could be added one papal appointee to represent the Pope, though this person would have no power of veto. There could be one bishop from each region (six), with the rest being non-bishops. The members chosen should be free to work full time on the Central Commission. Because of the great importance of this Commission to the entire work of the Council, the bishops would be asked to appoint the very best persons they have available. Every effort should be made to ensure that the Commission does not consist of eighteen men, but has the best possible gender balance.

The Central Commission would have the task of determining the detailed norms that would govern this Council and seeking the consent of the members of the

Council for these norms. Within these boundaries, the Central Commission would then determine all procedural questions and all questions relating to the time to be allotted to each question discussed by the Council and each stage of the process. It would determine the order in which the topics would be discussed, so that different topics can be brought to a vote at different times allowing the entire task of the Council to be gradually fulfilled. It would also have the task of coordinating the work of the Regional Commissions.

The Regional Commission

The members of the Council within the jurisdiction of each Bishops' Conference could establish an office in their region (the Regional Office) and elect, from the members of the Council or from outside it, a commission (the Regional Commission). This Regional Commission would determine the manner and timeline of the work of the Council to be carried out in that region, and would coordinate all such work.

Smaller Bishops' Conferences would be free to join with other Conferences, setting up one Regional Office and one Regional Commission for their combined area.

The Local Commission

Each member of the Council could publicly name a number of persons to work as a Local Commission in advising the member on all matters raised by the Council and in assisting in consulting the people of that area.

DETERMINING THE GENERAL TOPICS

In any human endeavour, if we want the right answers, we must first ask the right questions. Furthermore, if the statements expressing the questions are ambiguous or unclear or fail to address exactly the matter they are dealing with, great confusion will be caused. Time spent determining and refining the right questions will in the end save time and energy for the whole Council. It is, therefore, legitimate to spend considerable time on this aspect of the Council.

The process could begin with the Central Commission drawing up a list of those broad subject areas that they believe should be discussed and decided by the Council, and forwarding this list to the members throughout the world. I have suggested a number in this book, but I make no claim that my list is exhaustive and I know that other people will have other suggestions and/or refinements.

The 10 000 members of the Council could then consider the list of topics forwarded from the Central Commission and propose variations or additions. In doing this, they could, to the greatest extent possible, listen to the wisdom of the Church around them in their area and use members of the Local Commission in doing so. The changes the individual members propose would be sent to the Regional Office.

The members of the Council in that region would

consider the proposed variations and additions sent by individual members and vote on them, with only those that receive the support of two thirds of the members being forwarded to the Central Commission. This Central Commission would study the proposals from around the world and, in fidelity to the wishes of the members of the Council, decide on which topics to include.

DETERMINING THE PARTICULAR MATTERS FOR DISCUSSION AND VOTING

As soon as the general topics had been determined, the members of the Council could take up the work of determining the specific points to be voted on under each topic.

These points could be presented as statements expressed in one single sentence and containing one single idea, and could be framed in such a manner that they can be answered by a simple A = 'affirmative' (I endorse the statement), N = 'negative' (I disagree with the statement), U = 'unsure' (the arguments on both sides appear to be equal and I cannot decide between them) or D = 'defer' (the arguments given on both sides are not sufficiently mature and the matter should be deferred to a later Council).

More complex ideas should be divided into several statements. In framing them, matters of style should give way to clarity and substance. Needless to say, a series of consecutive statements could go together as part of an argument on a particular topic, but they would remain separate statements, to be voted on separately. They could be called simply 'the statements'.

All members of the Church could be invited to be part of this process in accordance with the principle that the process is at least as important as the written outcomes.

While any member of the Church could propose statements, those with a special expertise in a particular area would be asked to do so.

While any member of the church could send in proposals, it would be highly recommended that ideas be refined by discussion with larger groups before being presented. On the one hand, the larger the number of people involved in a discussion, the greater the attention that ought to be given to the submission; on the other hand, a carefully researched submission by an expert in a particular field might be worth far more than a more superficial discussion between many people. The aim would always be to receive the best ideas, while at the same time finding a balance between an invitation to all to participate and the need to limit the amount of time necessary to read and evaluate all the material submitted.

The only proposals that would be considered would be those that came in the form of the statements as described above.

The members of the Council in that region would then consider all the submissions made and draw up a list of statements under each topic. Only those statements that received the support of two thirds of the members would be forwarded to the Central Commission.

The Central Commission would then, by a majority vote, draw up a list from all the submissions received and send this out to the members of the Council.

REFINING THE QUESTIONS

So important is the matter of getting the questions right that a third stage of this process could take place in which the members of the Council—again perhaps in consultation with the community—may propose amendments to the wording of the statements. They would then forward their amendments to the Regional Office. A two-thirds majority of the members of the Council within a particular region would be required before a proposed amendment was forwarded to the Central Commission. A new statement could be proposed with the support of four fifths of the members within a particular region.

The Central Commission would then, by a majority vote, finalise the list of statements.

THE LEARNED SOCIETIES

Within the church in most countries there are societies of persons with an expertise in a particular field of church study, e.g. scripture scholars, historians, dogmatic theologians, moral theologians, canon lawyers etc. There are other groups of people who could also make an expert contribution in various fields, e.g. doctors, psychologists, lawyers, social workers etc., especially those with experience and expertise in the healing of victims, the treatment of offenders, professional codes of conduct, the prevention of abuse, protocols for the investigation of claims of abuse etc.

These societies could have their important role in the process of the Council, in line with the idea of an ongoing dialogue between the voting members of the Council and these experts on relevant topics. These societies or groups could be invited by the members of the Council in that region to discuss those statements that come within their own particular field of expertise. Seven tasks could then be assigned:

- to assist in the work of choosing the topics and preparing the statements under each topic
- to select among the statements those that they foresee will be more controversial and/or in which they feel that their own contribution will be most useful
- to discuss these controversial or key statements among themselves and thus inform themselves on these matters
- to prepare papers setting forth the major arguments for and against a particular statement and forward these papers to the members of the Council in their region, at the same time making the papers publicly available
- to be aware of significant contributions for or against the statements made in other countries and make appropriate use of them, though without overwhelming the members with more material than they could fairly be asked to study
- to make themselves available to meetings of the

members of the Council in their region for discussion of the questions

- to take a vote among themselves on all those statements that come within their field of expertise and to publish the results at a time determined by their Regional Commission, under the overall direction of the Central Commission.

When the learned society concerns a Church discipline (e.g. theology or scripture studies), appropriate members of other Christian Churches could be invited to join the discussions, with a right to vote, but perhaps with their votes counted separately.

When the society concerns a secular discipline (e.g. psychology or investigation of claims of abuse), religion would be irrelevant, both in regards to eligibility for membership and to voting.

The work of the learned societies could have one other function, in that all private opinions should first be submitted to these societies. The Catholic people of the world would then know that anyone who sought to publicise private views through the media without first presenting them to the learned societies was most probably someone who could not convince his or her own peers.

The Central Commission could have the right to forward to the members of the Council a limited amount of selected material on particular questions.

DISCUSSIONS

Each member of the Council could be encouraged to hold open discussions in the place where they live—either personally or though the members of the Local Commission—and invite input from any who wish to attend, always remembering that the process of the Council is just as important as the content.

At regional meetings the members of the Council could then discuss those questions that they believe most require such discussion. They could take provisional and informal votes on various questions in order to determine which ones need the most study and discussion. They could invite experts or representative groups to attend their discussions and assist through their expertise.

VOTING

At times determined by the Central Commission the voting on each topic would take place. Different parts of the entire work of the Council could be brought to a vote at different times.

The first step could be to gather the votes of the learned societies from around the world bearing on that topic, collate them and make public the results of the voting, so that the members of the Council might be aware of the opinions of the experts in each field.

At the appropriate time, the members of the Council would then be invited to vote and to forward their votes, by a suitable and secure means, to the Regional Office, which would count them and in turn forward them to the

Central Commission.

ASSESSMENT OF THE VOTING

To set a mark of 50% and then divide the votes into 'passed' and 'defeated' seems inadequate when speaking of faith, morals and church practice. There should surely be a difference between a statement that receives 52% support and another that receives 97% support. Rather than simply dividing the statements into those that are 'passed' and those that are 'defeated', each statement could be published together with the percentages of those favouring or opposing.

On a matter of faith or morals, one would look for a consensus rather than a simple majority. When a consensus has not been reached, the Central Commission could decide that certain statements need to be rephrased, then be resubmitted to the Council for further study and eventually for a new vote. Whenever possible, the Council would seek consensus.

In matters of Church practice, the Church may in some cases need to proceed on the basis of a bare majority, though even there it should always remember that a vote of 51% for and 49% against really means that the Church is divided down the middle and there is no agreement.

While adequate time must be allowed, the Central Commission would also have the task of ensuring that the work keeps moving and the Council does not last longer than necessary.

THE MIND OF THE CHURCH

When the work of the Council on a particular topic has been completed and the members of the Council have voted, the conclusions of the Council could be submitted to a vote of the entire Church; every person who has reached the age of eighteen years and has been baptised in, or received into, the Catholic Church could be eligible to vote. It could be determined that, before they could vote, they would have to register to vote according to norms established by the Bishops' Conference of that region. Each vote could be taken at Sunday Mass.

It would be neither possible nor desirable to invite the entire Church to vote on each single one of the possibly thousands of statements that would emerge from the Council. Instead, the Central Commission could group together a number, even a large number, of statements dealing with a particular topic and propose this group of statements to a single vote by all those eligible to vote. Where opportune, however, it could seek the vote of the entire Church on one particular statement. In all cases, the voting of both the experts and the members of the Council would be included with the proposal.

EXPENSES

There would, of course, be expenses associated with this Council, though they should be less than would be incurred by a traditional Council. One could anticipate that the Catholic people of the world would strongly support the idea of this Council and would be willing to contribute to a collection (or even several over a period of time) taken up for this purpose. Care would obviously have to be taken that lay members were not asked to contribute so much time without recompense that they would have inadequate time left over to support their families, for it would obviously be counterproductive if in this the Council were seen not to observe natural justice.

To avoid the destruction of a large forest, electronic communication could be preferred to the printing of hard copies.

Through the entire process set out in this chapter, one could surely hope that the mind of the Church concerning sexual abuse would emerge. One might hope that it would become clear that the Church was at last truly serious about banishing all shadow of sexual abuse, and that this would be the best evangelization it could possibly carry out.

ALSO BY BISHOP GEOFFREY ROBINSON
and available through Garratt Publishing

Confronting Power and Sex in the Catholic Church: Reclaiming the Spirit of Jesus

Drawing on his own experiences in responding to abuse, Bishop Geoffrey Robinson, in this explosive work, methodically offers a critique of the Church's use and misuse of power, from the Pope proclaiming infallibility down to the preacher claiming a divine authority for every word spoken from the pulpit. Going back to the Bible and, above all, to the teaching of Jesus, he presents an approach to sexual morality that is profound, compassionate and people-centred. He stresses the priority of the hierarchy of holiness over the hierarchy of power. He offers nothing less than a vision for a Church of the third millennium—a Church that wants to see its members take the responsibility appropriate to adults rather than obedience appropriate to children, and wants to help all people grow to become all they are capable of being. [ISBN 9781920721473]

Love's Urgent Longings: Wrestling with belief in today's Church

Love's Urgent Longings is the story of a journey. A spiritual journey made over the past few years by Bishop Geoffrey Robinson. In seeking for answers to the urgent longings of the title, he goes back to basics to encounter the spiritual, to consciously respond to the force of his deepest desires and to understand the ways that they move him towards higher goals. This sounds like a very personal journey, and so it is. However, it is also a journey that will resonate with a great many Catholics. Geoffrey Robinson's journey is your journey; it is our journey as a Church and as believers. His questions are your questions. Above all this is a positive story. Bishop Robinson is not trying to reject all that is past and, as he puts it 'construct a new building from the foundations up'. He does not wish to believe in nothing or become vaguely 'spiritual'. He says: 'If I must leave something behind, I want to do so only because I have found something of equal value to put in its place'. *Love's Urgent Longings* is a journey, a story, a testament, both a personal one and a dialogue with and for those, both old and young, who are wrestling with belief in today's Church. [ISBN 9781920682217]

The Gospel of Luke: For Meditation and Homilies

Geoffrey Robinson's commentary on the Gospel of Luke takes us on a fascinating journey into the mind of the evangelist. He extends an invitation to engage in the practice of *Lectio Divina*. Reading and meditating on scriptures with him can open us to new ways of listening to God. He examines the whole of Luke's Gospel, passage by passage, showing how Luke's way of telling it offers us possibilities of beginning to see and know God more deeply. This deep comprehension of the text unfolds Luke's extraordinary gift: showing Jesus' unique way of demonstrating God's astonishing love for imperfect, frightened, limited human beings. Robinson's glowing exposition shows us the endless compassion and insight of Jesus as seen by Luke. Ultimately, Robinson tells us, Jesus sang a song to each one of us; understanding more about Jesus in Luke helps us to sing Jesus' song ourselves.

[ISBN 9781921946349]

garratt PUBLISHING

Toll free: 1300 650 878
sales@garrattpublishing.com.au
www.garrattpublishing.com.au

CPSIA information can be obtained at www.ICGtesting.com
Printed in the USA
LVOW122359020713

341300LV00012B/217/P